Institutional Economics and Immigrant Integration

Daniel Rauhut

Institutional Economics and Immigrant Integration

How Informal Institutions Impact the Integration Process

palgrave
macmillan

Daniel Rauhut
Centre for Migration and Integration Studies
Lund, Sweden

ISBN 978-3-032-28360-3 ISBN 978-3-032-28361-0 (eBook)
https://doi.org/10.1007/978-3-032-28361-0

This Palgrave Macmillan imprint is published by the registered company Springer Nature Switzerland AG.
The registered company address is: Gewerbestrasse 11, 6330 Cham, Switzerland

Preface

The complexity of human behaviour has long captivated scholars across multiple disciplines. Numerous theories and frameworks have emerged to explain why humans behave as they do, alongside normative prescriptions for how they ought to behave. Psychologists and sociologists have traditionally dominated research into human behaviour, which is entirely understandable given the nature of their disciplines. It was towards the end of my undergraduate studies in Economic History that I first encountered Gary Becker's economic analysis of dating, mating, and family formation. This introduction subsequently led me to explore his broader economic analyses of human behaviour and the writings of Alessandro Cigno on the economics of the family. The mathematical formalization of human behaviour proved intellectually compelling. During my doctoral studies, I engaged extensively with the work of Amartya Sen, who similarly employed mathematical formalizations to explain the capabilities available to the poor and how these might be optimally utilized.

For many years, I have worked on immigrant integration from Swedish, Nordic, and European perspectives. Integration outcomes vary considerably: sometimes the process proceeds smoothly for both immigrants and host societies, whilst in other instances it fails to achieve intended objectives. This variability has occupied numerous scholars over time.

Between 2020 and 2022, I participated in an EU-funded project that analysed the social and economic impact of immigration to rural and mountainous regions in Europe. Several publications arising from this work laid the foundation for the present book. One paper examined how culture impacts immigrant integration, drawing on institutional economics (Rauhut 2020); others explored the methodological and epistemological trajectories of different integration theories (Rauhut, 2023), integration from a bordering perspective (Rauhut & Laine, 2023), and the economic consequences of immigration beyond urban centres (Rauhut et al., 2023). Subsequently, I authored a comprehensive appraisal and review of the main integration theories, examining their meanings and potential outcomes if implemented (Rauhut, 2026). This latter work serves as a bridge between the project-related publications from 2020 to 2023 and the present volume.

This book, firstly, should be understood primarily as an attempt to analyse and understand what role informal institutions, such as, e.g., norms, preferences, values, and other culturally determined influences, have on the process of immigrant integration. Institutional economics offers a valuable tool in this work. Secondly, it should be understood as a development of ideas advanced by Becker and other economists regarding the analysis of racism, discrimination, and human action and behaviour through economic theory and formalized mathematical models, extended here to encompass immigrant integration. The fundamental premise is that immigrants and natives are different. I recognize that researchers from other disciplines with different epistemological starting points may disagree with this premise. However, this differentiation does not imply that natives are superior and immigrants inferior; rather, the cultures, norms, preferences, and values held by natives and immigrants are analysed using a nominal rather than ordinal scale. A nominal scale categorizes data based on characteristics—consider colours (red, blue, green), types of fruit (apple, banana, orange), or vehicle types (car, truck, motorcycle)—where no category is deemed 'better' or 'worse' than another. An ordinal scale, by contrast, involves categories that can be ordered or ranked (such as customer satisfaction levels or educational attainment). Since all cultures are considered equal in this study, the nominal scale represents the natural analytical choice.

I wish to express my gratitude to the many colleagues and friends who have assisted me, whether directly or indirectly, through discussions, correspondence, or by reading drafts. Their comments, observations, and constructive criticism have proved invaluable. I am particularly indebted to Marika Gruber, Göran Adamson, Stuart Reid, Torben Dall Schmidt, Mary Ann Stamsø, and Per-Olav Lund for their contributions to this work. However, the inclusion of names in these acknowledgements does not imply that the individuals necessarily endorse the views expressed herein; their input is nonetheless gratefully acknowledged as they made me rethink or sharpen my arguments. Any remaining shortcomings are my responsibility alone. Lastly, I also want to thank Wyndham Hacket Pain, together with the Palgrave Macmillan production team.

This book is written with several audiences in mind. It will, I hope, be of interest to academics and postgraduate students working within disciplines concerned with immigrant integration and integration policy, including economics, political science, sociology, geography, law, history, and migration studies. Academic libraries and research institutions may likewise find the volume a useful resource. Beyond the academic sphere, the book is intended for stakeholders and practitioners engaged in the development and implementation of integration policies, particularly within the EU administration and the various levels of governance across Member States. The analytical approach adopted here may also prove valuable in postgraduate and advanced undergraduate courses that explore migration, regional development, social policy, and institutional economics.

It is my hope that this work contributes meaningfully to our understanding of immigrant integration by offering fresh analytical perspectives grounded in economic theory. If this book succeeds in advancing scholarly discourse on integration processes and informing evidence-based policy discussions, it will have fulfilled its purpose. The challenges of integration are too important—for immigrants, host societies, and policymakers alike—to be addressed without the rigorous analytical tools that economic theory can provide.

Lund, Sweden
March, 2026

Daniel Rauhut

Competing Interests The author has no competing interests to declare that are relevant to the content of this manuscript.

Contents

About the Author

Daniel Rauhut is an associate professor with a PhD in Economic History. Currently, he is the director of the independent research institute 'Centre for Migration and Integrations Studies', Lund, Sweden. He is also an Affiliated Researcher at the Centro de Estudos Geográficos, Universidade de Lisboa, Portugal, and a Research Associate at the Institute for Applied Research of Ageing, Villach, Austria.For over 25 years, he has addressed international migration and immigrant integration at universities in Sweden, Norway, and Finland, participating in numerous EU-funded research projects. His research focuses on EU social policies, labour market integration of immigrants, Swedish emigration to Portugal, and the socio-economic impact of third-country nationals in peripheral regions.He is a peer reviewer for more than 25 scientific journals, and he received an international research award in 2017. He co-edited *Poverty in the History of Economic Thought* (Routledge, 2020), *Poverty in Contemporary Economic Thought* (Routledge, 2021), *EU Cohesion Policy and Spatial Governance* (Edward Elgar, 2021), *Assessing the Social Impact of Immigration in Europe: Renegotiating Remoteness* (Edward Elgar, 2023), and *Inequality: Social and Economic Aspects* (Routledge, 2024). He also edited *New Methods and Theory on Immigrant Integration: Insights from Remote and Peripheral Areas* (Edward Elgar, 2023) and co-authored *The Economics of Immigration Beyond the Cities: Theoretical Perspectives and Empirical Insights* (Palgrave Macmillan, 2023). Recently, he co-edited *Refugee Housing in Europe: Challenges and Opportunities in Multi-dimensional Governance* (Edward Elgar, 2026), and authored *Immigrant Entrepreneurship in Sweden: Economic Perspectives* (Macmillan Palgrave, 2025).

List of Figures

CHAPTER 1

Introduction

Background

Imagine arriving in a new country where a simple nod might be interpreted as rude dismissal, where your professional qualifications suddenly become worthless pieces of paper, and where your children begin to speak a language that feels foreign in your own home. This is the lived reality of cultural distance, a phenomenon that transforms the universal human experience of migration into something far more complex and consequential than mere geographical relocation.

Cultural differences have always been humanity's most enduring signature, shaping everything from intimate dinner conversations to the grand theatre of international diplomacy. Every human society develops its own distinctive cultural DNA, i.e., a unique combination of values, beliefs, practices, and worldviews that provides meaning and structure to social life (Geertz, 1973). Yet these very patterns that bind communities together simultaneously create invisible walls that can complicate relationships between groups carrying different cultural repertoires.

But how exactly do these cultural differences wield their influence over human relations? The answer lies in surprisingly mundane moments. Consider Edward T. Hall's discovery that entire cultures can be categorized by how much context they pack into their communication (Hall, 1976). In high-context cultures, a pause, a gesture, or what remains unsaid carries enormous weight. In low-context cultures, directness and explicit

D. Rauhut, *Institutional Economics and Immigrant Integration*,
https://doi.org/10.1007/978-3-032-28361-0_1

communication are prized. When these styles collide, say, in a job interview or a parent-teacher conference, the potential for systematic misunderstanding becomes enormous, even among the most well-intentioned people.

The stakes become even higher when we venture into the territory of fundamental values. What happens when one person's definition of individual freedom directly contradicts another's understanding of family obligation? Ronald Inglehart's extensive research across societies reveals that these are not merely differences of opinion; rather, they represent entirely different ways of seeing the world that influence everything from voting patterns to parenting styles (Inglehart, 1997). These worldview differences create fault lines that can fracture communities when they are not carefully navigated.

Perhaps most troubling is how quickly neutral differences can transform into sources of social tension. Henri Tajfel and John Turner's *Social Identity Theory* demonstrates that humans possess an almost uncanny ability to create in-groups and out-groups from the thinnest of distinctions (Tajfel & Turner, 1979). When these arbitrary divisions align with meaningful cultural differences, the results can be explosive. Suddenly, the way someone dresses, prays, or raises their children becomes a marker of belonging or otherness that influences trust, cooperation, and social cohesion across entire communities.

Yet this story need not end in conflict. Gordon Allport's contact hypothesis, supported by decades of subsequent research, reveals that positive intercultural contact can indeed bridge these divides (Allport, 1954). Thomas Pettigrew and Linda Tropp's analysis of over 500 studies confirms that intergroup contact generally reduces prejudice, though the devil, as always, lies in the details of how, when, and where this contact occurs (Pettigrew & Tropp, 2006).

When Movement Changes Everything

Migration fundamentally alters this delicate dance of cultural difference. When people cross borders, they do not simply encounter different cultural practices; they step into entire institutional universes built upon different cultural assumptions. The friendly neighbourhood doctor's surgery, the local primary school, the job centre, each operates according to cultural logic that may be completely foreign to newcomers.

This transformation occurs through several powerful mechanisms. First, migrants typically arrive as numerical minorities lacking the social networks, institutional knowledge, and political representation that established residents take for granted. This creates what scholars call asymmetrical power relations, where cultural differences cease to be neutral variations and become hierarchical distinctions between 'mainstream' and 'other' cultures.

Pierre Bourdieu's concept of 'cultural capital' becomes painfully relevant here (Bourdieu, 1986). The accumulated knowledge, credentials, and practices that made someone successful in their home country may suddenly become worthless, or worse, sources of disadvantage, in their new environment. A renowned surgeon finds herself cleaning offices; a respected teacher drives a taxi. The institutional machinery of the host society does not simply ignore their cultural capital; it actively devalues it.

Meanwhile, the migration experience itself creates unique psychological pressures that compound these challenges. John Berry's influential framework on acculturation strategies reveals that immigrants face impossible choices about cultural maintenance vs. adaptation that can profoundly affect both individual wellbeing and broader integration outcomes (Berry, 1997). Should they preserve their children's heritage language at the risk of academic disadvantage? Should they adopt local social customs that feel morally uncomfortable? These are not merely personal preferences; they are strategic decisions with lasting consequences.

The Evolution of Understanding

How scholars have attempted to understand these dynamics tells a fascinating story of intellectual evolution and ongoing debate. Classical assimilation theory, born from observations of early twentieth-century American immigration, painted integration as a largely linear journey from cultural otherness to mainstream acceptance (Park & Burgess, 1921). Milton Gordon's influential elaboration distinguished between cultural and structural assimilation, arguing that immigrants must first abandon their cultural distinctiveness before achieving full institutional participation (Gordon, 1964). This 'melting pot' vision profoundly shaped both academic thinking and policy approaches for decades.

Yet this tidy narrative began to unravel as scholars observed more complex patterns of integration. Neo-assimilation theorists like Richard Alba and Victor Nee acknowledged greater complexity whilst maintaining that cultural convergence remained central to successful integration (Alba & Nee, 2003). They painted a more nuanced picture, i.e., integration might be bumpy and nonlinear, but cultural adaptation remained the ultimate destination.

The co-existence paradigm emerged as a direct challenge to these assumptions. Philosophers like Will Kymlicka argued that cultural maintenance and host society integration were not mutually exclusive but could flourish simultaneously under appropriate conditions (Kymlicka, 1996). Tariq Modood's analysis of Muslim communities in Europe demonstrated how religious and cultural identities could be maintained while achieving remarkable educational and economic success, fundamentally challenging assumptions about the necessity of cultural convergence (Modood, 2007).

Alejandro Portes and Min Zhou complicated the picture further with their segmented assimilation theory, which recognized that different groups might follow entirely distinct integration pathways depending on their reception context and community characteristics (Portes & Zhou, 1993). Suddenly, the question was not whether cultural distance mattered, but how it interacted with structural factors to produce different outcomes for different people in different places.

Critical theorists pushed back against all these approaches, arguing that focusing on cultural adaptation obscured more fundamental issues of structural discrimination and power asymmetries. Post-colonial perspectives emphasized how immigration and integration processes were embedded within broader histories of colonialism and global inequality that could not be solved through cultural adjustment alone (Bhabha, 1994).

Constructivist approaches added yet another layer of complexity by questioning whether cultural distance was a fixed characteristic at all. Andreas Wimmer's work on ethnic boundary-making demonstrated how cultural differences could become salient or irrelevant depending on institutional contexts and political dynamics (Wimmer, 2008). Perhaps cultural distance was not something that people carried with them like luggage, but something that emerged from social interaction itself.

The Persistent Puzzle

Despite this rich theoretical development, several critical limitations persist. The fragmentation of scholarly approaches has created academic tribes that often speak past each other, with assimilationists, multiculturalists, and critical theorists operating from fundamentally different assumptions about the nature of culture, integration, and social change. This fragmentation limits both theoretical progress and practical application of research findings.

More troubling is the limited predictive power of existing theories. While each tradition offers valuable insights, none provides adequate tools for predicting which immigrants in which contexts will experience which types of integration outcomes. This limitation stems partly from the lack of precise conceptualization and measurement of cultural distance itself, which has remained frustratingly impressionistic despite its central importance.

Perhaps most critically, the disconnect between theoretical sophistication and policy relevance has left policymakers with limited practical guidance. Current approaches often resort to either crude assimilationist policies that ignore cultural diversity or superficial multiculturalist policies that sidestep genuine cultural conflicts. The development of more precise, measurable, and policy-relevant theoretical frameworks represents not just an academic challenge, but an urgent societal need as nations worldwide struggle with unprecedented levels of cultural diversity.

The story of cultural distance in immigration is ultimately a story about the fundamental challenge of living together across difference. As migration continues to reshape societies globally, our ability to understand and navigate these dynamics will determine whether cultural diversity becomes a source of enrichment or division. The stakes could not be higher, and the need for better theoretical tools has never been more pressing.

Cultural Differences as Informal Institutions

The relationship between cultural differences and immigrant integration can be understood through the lens of institutional economics, which provides a robust theoretical framework for analysing how informal institutions shape economic behaviour and social outcomes. This perspective reveals important connections between cultural distance, institutional theory, and integration processes that merit careful examination. Culture and consequently cultural distance are fundamentally rooted in informal institutions. North (1991) distinguished between formal institutions, such as laws and regulations, and informal institutions, which encompass the norms, values, beliefs, customs, and social conventions that guide human behaviour. Social interaction and preferences of codes of conduct, what is socially acceptable or not, and customs and traditions are determined by informal institutions in society (Milgrom et al., 1990; March & Olsen, 1986). Informal institutions, as North (1990, p. 40) notes, include codes of conduct, norms of behaviour, and conventions as well as extensions, elaborations and modifications of formal rules, and 'are a part of the heritage that we call culture'. This is a clarification of the definition given by March and Olsen (1989). Cultural distance essentially measures the extent to which these informal institutional frameworks differ between societies or groups (Kingston & Caballero, 2009).

When examining immigrant populations and host societies, cultural distance reflects variations in deeply embedded social norms, value systems, and behavioural expectations as well as the integration outcomes (Penninx, 2003). Religion plays an important role here; the reason why the West grew rich is related to the dissolvement of religious influences over politics and economics (Rosenberg & Birdzell Jr, 1986). The rise of a strong state and codified laws are other key institutions shaping the institutions of the West (North & Thomas, 1973), as are individualism, women's rights, LGBTQ+ rights, etc. (Goldin, 2021; Alesina et al., 2013; OECD, 2024).

These informal institutions exert considerable influence on immigrant integration outcomes across multiple dimensions. The process of integration involves not merely legal or administrative adjustments, but fundamental adaptations to different ways of organizing social and economic life. Informal institutions affect how immigrants navigate labour markets, form social networks, establish trust relationships, and engage with both formal and informal economic activities. When cultural distance is substantial, meaning that informal institutions differ markedly between origin and destination societies, integration becomes more challenging and typically requires longer timeframes to achieve (Rauhut, 2020). This occurs because immigrants must learn, adapt to, or negotiate between competing sets of informal rules and expectations whilst simultaneously navigating formal institutional requirements. However, an adjustment process is also required from the host country and its residents.

Challenges

Picture a sixteen-year-old girl sitting at her family's dinner table, caught between two worlds that seem increasingly irreconcilable. Her parents speak of honour, tradition, and the importance of family reputation, whilst her teachers and friends champion individual choice, personal freedom, and self-expression. Each morning, she must decide which version of herself to present to the world, and each evening, she returns home feeling like a stranger in her own skin. This is the lived reality of cultural distance in many immigrant families, where abstract academic concepts translate into profound personal struggles that can last generations.

The intersection of cultural distance and immigrant integration creates a complex web of challenges that ripple outwards from individual hearts and minds to reshape entire communities and societies. These are not merely statistical problems to be solved by policy wonks but represent the daily struggles of millions of people worldwide who must navigate between different cultural systems with potentially incompatible demands and expectations.

When Identity Becomes a Battlefield

The most profound challenges arising from cultural distance are intensely personal, touching the very core of who people believe themselves to be. Psychologists have coined the term 'acculturative stress' to describe the unique form of psychological distress that emerges when people must navigate between different cultural systems (Berry, 2006). However, this clinical term barely captures the emotional turmoil experienced by someone whose fundamental beliefs about right and wrong, appropriate and inappropriate, sacred and mundane are suddenly called into question by their new environment.

The psychological literature reveals how large cultural distances can fragment identity and create lasting confusion, particularly among second-generation immigrants who inherit these conflicts as their birthright (Phinney, 1990). Alejandro Portes and Rubén Rumbaut's longitudinal research following immigrant families across decades shows how cultural distance can turn the natural tensions between parents and children into something far more destructive, i.e., battles over fundamental values that can tear families apart (Portes & Rumbaut, 2001). Children may find themselves serving as cultural translators not just linguistically, but morally and socially, bearing burdens that no child should carry.

But the challenges do not end with successful cultural adaptation. Homi Bhabha's concept of 'mimicry' reveals a cruel paradox: immigrants who successfully adapt to their new culture may find that their very success marks them as perpetually foreign (Bhabha, 1994). They become almost-but-not-quite authentic members of their new society, trapped in what sociologists call 'segmented inclusion', i.e., formally accepted but culturally othered, citizens on paper but strangers in practice.

When Communities Fragment

These individual struggles aggregate into community-level challenges that can fundamentally alter the social fabric of entire neighbourhoods and cities. Robert Putnam's research on diversity and social capital delivered an uncomfortable truth: ethnic diversity, particularly when associated with large cultural distances, can initially reduce social trust and civic engagement (Putnam, 2007). Suddenly, the local community centre that once buzzed with shared activities becomes a patchwork of separate groups, each speaking their own language and following their own customs.

The spatial dimension of these challenges creates what researchers euphemistically call 'residential segregation patterns', but what residents experience as increasingly isolated communities where crossing the street can feel like crossing cultural boundaries. Sako Musterd's analysis of European cities reveals how cultural distance interacts with economic factors to create persistent ethnic clustering that becomes self-reinforcing over time (Musterd, 2005). Limited contact perpetuates stereotypes and misunderstandings whilst reducing opportunities for the kind of meaningful relationships that could bridge cultural divides.

These patterns can create what critics describe as 'parallel societies', i.e., communities that exist side by side but rarely intersect, like strangers sharing the same postal code but inhabiting different worlds. The corner shops may serve different foods, the community centres may host different celebrations, and the schools may struggle to create shared experiences that resonate with children from vastly different cultural backgrounds.

Institutional Battlegrounds

Perhaps nowhere are these challenges more visible than in the institutions that structure daily life, e.g., schools, workplaces, and political systems that often seem designed for cultural homogeneity rather than diversity. Educational systems find themselves caught between competing cultural models of learning, authority, and family involvement that can make the simple act of teaching extraordinarily complex.

Consider the cultural collision that occurs when parents from hierarchical educational traditions, where teachers are revered figures who should never be questioned, encounter progressive educational systems that expect parental involvement, student participation, and critical thinking. John Ogbu and Herbert Simons' research on voluntary vs. involuntary minorities reveals how these different cultural models of education can significantly influence academic outcomes, creating achievement gaps that persist across generations (Ogbu & Simons, 1998).

The workplace presents its own battlefield of cultural expectations and professional norms. Beyond the obvious challenges of credential recognition, cultural distance affects everything from hiring decisions to promotion opportunities through mechanisms so subtle they often go unnoticed. Devah Pager and Hana Shepherd's audit study research demonstrates how cultural markers, e.g., names, accents, religious dress, social customs, can influence employment outcomes independently of qualifications or experience (Pager & Shepherd, 2008). A highly qualified engineer may find herself perpetually passed over for promotion not because she lacks technical skills, but because her communication style or social interactions do not match cultural expectations about leadership.

Political participation presents perhaps the most complex institutional challenge. When immigrants arrive with different understandings of citizen-state relationships, i.e., perhaps viewing government as something to be avoided rather than engaged with, or expecting political participation to follow different cultural protocols, their integration into democratic institutions becomes fraught with misunderstanding. Irene Bloemraad's comparative research reveals how these cultural differences in political engagement can shape integration outcomes for entire communities (Bloemraad, 2006).

The Ripple Effects: When Challenges Spread

These integration challenges do not remain contained within immigrant communities; they spread outwards to reshape the political, economic, and social landscape of entire societies. Understanding these wider impacts helps explain why immigration has become such a lightning rod for political conflict and why cultural distance has emerged as a central concern in democratic societies worldwide.

Political Earthquakes

The rise of populist movements across Western democracies cannot be understood without understanding the perceived cultural threats and the politics of cultural distance. Pippa Norris and Ronald Inglehart's analysis of populist support across multiple countries reveals that cultural backlash against immigration often trumps economic concerns in explaining voting patterns (Norris & Inglehart, 2019). This is not simply xenophobia or prejudice; it reflects genuine anxiety about social cohesion and shared values that mainstream political parties have often been reluctant to address directly.

The polarization of immigration policy debates reflects deeper fault lines about cultural diversity, national identity, and what it means to belong to a democratic society. John Sides, Michael Tesler, and Lynn Vavreck's analysis of American political polarization shows how immigration attitudes have become increasingly aligned with partisan identity, making evidence-based policy development more difficult whilst raising the stakes of getting cultural distance analysis right (Sides et al., 2018).

Even more troubling is the potential threat to democratic legitimacy itself. When large-scale immigration involving significant cultural distance generates persistent conflicts over fundamental values and social arrangements, the very foundations of democratic consensus can be shaken. Will Kymlicka's later work documents how cultural distance concerns have led to policy reversals and retreat from multiculturalism in several Western democracies, suggesting that democratic societies' capacity to manage cultural diversity may be more fragile than earlier frameworks assumed (Kymlicka, 2010).

Economic Aftershocks

The economic consequences of integration challenges create costs that extend far beyond individual immigrant experiences. When cultural distance impedes full economic integration, society loses the potential contributions of human capital that remains underutilized or misdirected. George Borjas' analysis of immigrant economic assimilation patterns shows how cultural factors can influence the speed and extent of economic convergence, with implications that ripple through fiscal systems and economic growth patterns (Borjas, 1999, 2019). In the *Culture Transplant*, Garett Jones shows that immigrants bring cultural attitudes from their homelands, towards saving, towards trust, and towards the role of government, that persist for decades, and likely for centuries, in their new national homes. The cultural attitudes Jones (2022) discusses are informal institutions, and they have enduring effects upon a nation's economic potential. His conclusion is that the informal institutions immigration brings will transform the economic, political, and social institutions of the receiving country.

These challenges can persist across generations, creating what economists call deadweight losses, i.e., resources consumed in managing integration difficulties rather than contributing to productive economic activity. Increased social service utilization, remedial education costs, and criminal justice expenditures associated with integration difficulties represent investments that yield limited returns whilst reducing the net economic benefits of immigration.

The geographic clustering of different immigrant communities can create regional economic disparities that exacerbate existing inequalities whilst generating new political tensions. Areas with high concentrations of culturally distant immigrants may face different economic challenges than more homogeneous regions, creating spatial mismatches between labour supply and demand that affect entire metropolitan areas.

Social Fabric Under Strain

Perhaps the most diffuse but potentially most significant impacts occur at the level of social fabric itself. Changing neighbourhood dynamics affect not only immigrants but established residents who must adapt to new forms of diversity in their immediate environments. The social psychology literature reveals that these changes can produce either positive outcomes through increased familiarity and reduced prejudice, or negative outcomes through increased competition and threat perception, depending critically on the conditions under which intercultural contact occurs (Pettigrew, 1998).

Generational differences in attitudes towards cultural diversity add another layer of complexity. Ronald Inglehart's research suggests that younger cohorts in Western societies are generally more accepting of cultural diversity, but this trend can be disrupted by rapid demographic change or economic insecurity (Inglehart, 2018). Understanding how cultural distance effects vary across generations becomes crucial for predicting long-term social trajectories.

Media representation plays a crucial role in amplifying or diminishing these challenges. Robert Entman and Andrew Rojecki's analysis of media coverage shows how news stories can amplify perceived cultural distances whilst providing limited context for understanding integration processes (Entman & Rojecki, 2000). These representational dynamics create feedback loops that can make cultural distance challenges more difficult to address through policy interventions.

The Policy Puzzle: Why Good Intentions Are Not Enough

Translating awareness of cultural distance challenges into effective policy responses reveals fundamental limitations in current approaches to immigrant integration. These are not merely technical problems requiring better implementation; they reflect deeper conceptual and political difficulties in managing cultural diversity within democratic frameworks.

The One-Size-Fits-All Trap

Current policy approaches suffer from a fundamental mismatch between the complexity of cultural distance effects and the simplicity of policy responses. Most integration policies treat immigrants as a homogeneous population requiring similar interventions, despite overwhelming evidence that integration processes vary dramatically depending on origin countries, cultural backgrounds, and reception contexts. A Syrian refugee fleeing civil war faces entirely different challenges than a Japanese executive relocating for career advancement, yet both may be channelled through identical integration programmes.

This policy uniformity reflects both political necessities, acknowledging cultural differences risk accusations of discrimination, and theoretical poverty. Without frameworks that can guide differentiated policy responses, policymakers retreat to the safety of universal approaches that may help no one particularly well.

The Measurement Mirage

Perhaps more troubling is the absence of reliable tools for measuring cultural distance itself. Policymakers routinely discuss cultural integration and cultural distance, yet they lack instruments for assessing these phenomena or evaluating policy effectiveness. This measurement gap means that policy debates often rely on impressionistic evidence and political rhetoric rather than systematic analysis of what works, for whom, and under what circumstances (Macuchova & Rauhut, 2023).

Existing integration policies focus heavily on easily measurable outcomes, e.g., language proficiency, employment rates, educational attainment, whilst paying limited attention to cultural adaptation processes that may be equally important for long-term integration success. This emphasis on structural indicators reflects both their measurability and political palatability but may miss crucial dimensions of integration that relate to social cohesion and democratic citizenship.

Political Tightrope Walking

The political constraints surrounding cultural distance create additional challenges for policy development. Democratic politics in diverse societies requires building coalitions across different cultural groups, making it politically risky to acknowledge cultural conflicts or implement policies that might appear to favour some groups over others. The result is often policy approaches that avoid discussing cultural distance directly whilst implementing measures that implicitly assume its importance.

The tension between integration goals and multicultural values creates persistent policy dilemmas. Policies emphasizing cultural adaptation risk criticism as assimilationist and discriminatory, whilst policies celebrating cultural diversity may be attacked for undermining social cohesion and shared citizenship. Threading this needle requires theoretical frameworks that can specify when cultural adaptation is necessary for integration and when cultural maintenance remains compatible with full societal participation.

Implementation Reality Check

Even well-designed policies face implementation challenges that reflect the complexity of cultural distance effects. Effective interventions often require coordination across multiple policy domains, e.g., education, employment, housing, social services, and levels of government, creating implementation demands that exceed the capacity of many existing institutional arrangements.

The professional expertise required to understand and address cultural distance effects may be lacking in many policy contexts. Training teachers, social workers, employment counsellors, and other frontline professionals to work effectively across large cultural distances requires investments in human capital that many jurisdictions are reluctant or unable to make.

These challenges collectively reveal why cultural distance has emerged as such a persistent concern in immigrant-receiving societies. The stakes are simultaneously deeply personal, touching individual identity and family relationships, and broadly societal, affecting democratic governance, economic performance, and social cohesion. Understanding these challenges in their full complexity is essential for developing more effective theoretical frameworks and policy responses that can help societies navigate the opportunities and pitfalls of cultural diversity in an increasingly mobile world.

What This Book Is About

Research Aim and Central Argument

This monograph addresses the theoretical and practical challenges outlined above by developing a comprehensive framework for understanding, measuring, and responding to cultural distance in immigrant integration processes. The primary aim is to construct a theoretical framework that synthesizes insights from multiple disciplinary traditions while providing the precision and policy relevance that existing approaches lack. It has been named the Cultural Distance Integration Model (CDIM). This model represents a departure from previous theoretical work in its emphasis on mathematical formalization, threshold effects, and mechanism-specific analysis that can inform targeted policy interventions.

The central argument of this work is that cultural distance operates as a measurable phenomenon with identifiable threshold effects that influence integration outcomes through specific mechanisms operating at individual, community, and institutional levels. Rather than treating cultural distance as an impressionistic concept or a simple linear variable, this framework proposes that cultural distance effects follow predictable patterns that can be mathematically modelled to enhance both theoretical understanding and policy effectiveness. The model posits that integration challenges and opportunities vary systematically with the magnitude of cultural distance, but that these relationships are mediated by contextual factors, institutional arrangements, and policy interventions that can be optimized through evidence-based approaches.

The CDIM framework builds upon Granovetter's concept of threshold models in social phenomena, applying this insight to cultural integration processes (Granovetter, 1978). Just as Granovetter demonstrated that individual decisions to participate in collective action depend on the number of others already participating, the CDIM argues that cultural integration processes exhibit threshold effects where small changes in cultural distance can produce disproportionately large changes in integration outcomes once critical thresholds are crossed.

Furthermore, the sociological and anthropological emphasis on meaning and identity has dominated the study of cultural difference, particularly in the context of migration and integration. However, this book draws inspiration from a more formal tradition of inquiry, one that treats cultural phenomena not merely as fluid narratives, but as structured systems governed by incentives, constraints, and equilibrium logics. A key inspiration for this book is the formal approach championed by Gary S. Becker in economics and sociology. The groundbreaking works by him exemplified how mathematically structured models could penetrate domains traditionally resistant to economic reasoning. His treatment of race relations, family dynamics, and social behaviour as systems of incentives and constraints, rather than as purely normative or cultural expressions, shifted the boundary between descriptive sociology and analytical modelling (Becker, 1957; Becker, 1976; Becker, 1991).

Moreover, the bidirectional nature of cultural distance effects represents another key component of the central argument. Unlike traditional assimilation models that focus primarily on immigrant adaptation, or co-existence and multiculturalism models that emphasize cultural maintenance, the CDIM recognizes that cultural distance affects both immigrant and host society populations through dynamic interaction processes. This bidirectional perspective draws on social psychological research on mutual intergroup differentiation and accommodation (Giles et al., 1991) but extends this insight to broader integration processes affecting entire communities and institutional systems.

Research Questions

The theoretical framework developed in this monograph addresses one overarching research question and several subsidiary questions that guide the analysis across multiple chapters. The primary research question asks: How can cultural distance be conceptualized, measured, and integrated into a comprehensive theoretical framework that explains immigrant integration outcomes and informs effective policy interventions? This question reflects the dual theoretical and practical objectives of the work, emphasizing both scholarly contribution and policy relevance.

The first subsidiary research question examines the mechanisms through which cultural distance affects integration processes: What are the key mechanisms through which cultural distance affects integration processes at different societal levels, and how do these mechanisms interact to produce observable integration outcomes? This question motivates the detailed analysis of individual-level psychological processes, community-level social dynamics, and institutional-level adaptation challenges that form the empirical foundation of the CDIM framework. The question assumes that integration outcomes result from complex interactions among multiple mechanisms rather than simple direct effects of cultural distance.

The second subsidiary question addresses theoretical positioning and gap identification: How do existing theoretical traditions in immigrant integration studies address cultural distance, and where are the critical gaps that require theoretical innovation? This question guides the comprehensive review of assimilationist, co-existence, critical, and constructivist approaches to integration, identifying both their contributions and their limitations for understanding cultural distance effects. The analysis reveals that while each tradition offers important insights, none provides adequate tools for predicting integration outcomes or designing targeted interventions.

The third question focuses on mathematical formalization and predictive modelling: What threshold effects exist in cultural distance impacts, and how can these be mathematically formalized to enable quantitative analysis and prediction of integration outcomes? This question reflects the monograph's commitment to moving beyond qualitative description towards quantitative modelling that can support evidence-based policy development. The mathematical formalization draws on complexity theory, network analysis, and dynamic systems modelling to capture the nonlinear and context-dependent nature of cultural distance effects.

The fourth question addresses theoretical synthesis and positioning: How can the Cultural Distance Integration Model be positioned within and contribute to existing theoretical traditions while addressing their limitations and extending their insights? This question recognizes that theoretical innovation builds upon existing knowledge while requiring careful positioning to demonstrate both continuity and advancement. The CDIM framework is designed to synthesize rather than replace existing theoretical insights while providing greater precision and policy relevance.

The final subsidiary question focuses on policy translation and implementation: What policy implications emerge from a threshold-based, mechanism-specific approach to cultural distance in integration, and how can these insights be translated into actionable policy frameworks? This question reflects the monograph's commitment to policy relevance and practical application. The analysis develops what we term 'precision integration policies' that adapt interventions to specific cultural distance levels and contextual factors rather than applying uniform approaches across all immigrant populations.

Methodological Approach

The methodological approach employed in this monograph combines theoretical synthesis, mathematical formalization, and policy analysis to develop a comprehensive understanding of cultural distance in immigrant integration. This multi-method approach reflects the complexity of the phenomenon under investigation and the need to bridge disciplinary boundaries to achieve theoretical innovation (Hall, 2020).

Theoretical synthesis represents the foundational methodological component, involving systematic analysis of existing literature across anthropology, sociology, psychology, political science, and economics to identify convergent insights and persistent gaps. This synthesis goes beyond simple literature review to engage in what Swedberg terms 'theorizing', the creative process of developing new theoretical insights through systematic engagement with existing knowledge (Swedberg, 2014). The synthesis identifies common mechanisms and patterns across different theoretical traditions while highlighting contradictions and limitations that motivate theoretical innovation.

Mathematical formalization constitutes the most distinctive methodological component of the work, translating theoretical insights into quantitative models that can generate testable predictions and inform policy design. This approach draws on recent developments in computational social science and complexity theory to model social phenomena that exhibit nonlinear dynamics and emergent properties (Miller & Page,

2007). The mathematical models developed here are designed to capture threshold effects, feedback loops, and contextual variation that characterize cultural distance impacts on integration processes.

The mathematical formalization employs several specific techniques adapted from different disciplinary traditions. Threshold models from sociology are used to capture discontinuous effects of cultural distance on integration outcomes. Granovetter's model of collective behaviour laid the groundwork for analysing how small shifts in individual conditions can produce large-scale social tipping points (Granovetter, 1978), while Macy and Evtushenko's more recent elaboration demonstrated the unpredictability that arises from heterogeneous threshold distributions (Macy & Evtushenko, 2020). Network analysis techniques are employed to model how cultural distance affects social capital formation and community-level integration processes. Bonding and bridging ties structure migrant integration opportunities and mediate exposure to host society norms (Kindler et al., 2015; Garip, 2008; Lőrincz & Németh, 2022). Dynamic systems modelling approaches from psychology are used to capture temporal dynamics and generational effects in cultural adaptation processes. Thelen and Smith's (1994) framework for cognitive development and Witherington's (2007) metatheoretical synthesis provide robust tools for modelling nonlinear, multi-level change processes relevant to immigrant generational adaptation.

The mathematical formalization of cultural distance and integration outcomes in this book echoes Becker's approach in several ways: first, it models social phenomena with economic logic. Like Becker, integration is treated not just as a sociological or normative issue, but as a system of incentives, constraints, and equilibria. Second, intangible variables are quantified. Becker modelled preferences, prejudice, and family decision-making; you model cultural distance, adaptation thresholds, and policy responsiveness. Third, policy relevance. Becker's work influenced welfare design and labour market regulation. The CDIM framework offers precision tools for integration policy calibration, especially in multicultural democracies.

Following this tradition, the Cultural Distance Integration Model (CDIM) applies Becker's logic to integration theory, modelling cultural differences as structured inputs in a system of social incentives, bounded rationalities, and institutional responses. Just as Becker quantified preferences and prejudices to explore labour market outcomes, this framework formalizes cultural distance, across civilizational, dimensional, and developmental levels, as a measurable variable capable of producing threshold effects in adaptation and policy success. The decision to translate cultural distance into mathematical form is thus not merely technical; it is a methodological continuation of Becker's conviction that even value-laden social behaviour can be modelled with precision, subjected to empirical testing, and used as the basis for policy optimization.

Policy analysis represents the third major methodological component, involving systematic examination of existing policy approaches and development of alternative frameworks based on the theoretical insights generated through synthesis and formalization (Bardach & Patashnik, 2020). This analysis employs comparative case study methodology to examine how different national contexts have addressed cultural distance challenges, identifying successful approaches and persistent problems that inform policy recommendations.

The policy analysis is informed by implementation science approaches that recognize the importance of translating theoretical insights into practical interventions that can be successfully implemented within existing institutional constraints (Fixsen et al., 2005). This perspective emphasizes the need to consider political feasibility, institutional capacity, and resource constraints in developing policy recommendations.

This book analyses cultures according to a nominal scale, where categories are labelled but not ranked. Unlike an ordinal scale, which implies hierarchy, progression, or superiority (e.g., beginner, intermediate, advanced), a nominal scale treats each category as distinct and equal in status (Rubin & Babbie, 2014). Everyday examples include hair colour (black, brown, red, blond, white) and fruit types (apples, oranges, kiwis, grapes, plums), where no inherent order or value is assigned to the categories. By applying this approach, CDIM makes no assumption that one culture is better, more evolved, or more desirable than another. The focus is on difference, not dominance.

In sum, the methodological architecture of this monograph reflects a deliberate fusion of classic social theory, contemporary modelling techniques, and policy responsiveness. By situating cultural distance within a formal system of predictive relationships and mechanism-specific effects, the CDIM departs from impressionistic theorizing and enters a Beckerian tradition of social analysis, one in which modelling does not strip away complexity but offers structured clarity within it.

Scope and Limitations

While this book aims to provide a comprehensive framework for understanding cultural distance in immigrant integration, it is important to acknowledge its scope and limitations to set appropriate expectations for readers and identify directions for future research. The geographic focus is primarily on Western democratic societies with significant immigration flows and established policy frameworks for managing diversity. This focus includes the European Union countries, the United States, Canada, Australia, and New Zealand, which share certain institutional features and democratic norms but also exhibit significant variation in integration approaches and outcomes.

Two important terminological distinctions require clarification for readers from different regional contexts. First, throughout this work, the term 'native' refers specifically to established populations in European receiving societies and should not be confused with its usage in North American or Australasian contexts, where 'native' typically denotes indigenous populations with distinct legal and historical status. In the European context employed here, 'native' simply refers to the existing population of the receiving country, regardless of their own historical migration background. Second, this analysis focuses primarily on immigration from outside the European Union. Under the 1992 Maastricht Treaty and subsequent European Union legislation, citizens of one EU member state who reside in another EU member state are not classified as 'immigrants' in legal terms but rather as 'EU citizens' exercising their right to freedom of movement; their civic rights are the same as in the country of citizenship (Mügge & van der Haar, 2016; European Commission, n.d.). While such individuals may still experience cultural distance effects when moving between EU countries with different languages and cultural traditions, their legal status and institutional rights differ fundamentally from those of third-country nationals (non-EU citizens), and they are therefore not the primary focus of this analysis.

The temporal scope emphasizes contemporary immigration patterns from approximately 1990 to the present, a period characterized by increased global mobility, changing migration patterns, and evolving approaches to integration policy. While historical examples are used to illustrate theoretical points, the framework is designed primarily for understanding current and future integration challenges rather than historical analysis of past migration waves.

The theoretical scope focuses specifically on cultural rather than structural integration barriers, though the framework recognizes that these dimensions interact in complex ways. Structural factors such as labour market discrimination, residential segregation, and institutional barriers receive attention insofar as they interact with cultural distance effects, but they are not the primary focus of analysis. This emphasis reflects both the distinctive contribution of the work and the need for analytical focus rather than comprehensive coverage of all integration factors.

The policy scope assumes democratic governance contexts with some commitment to managing cultural diversity through public policy interventions. The framework may have limited applicability in contexts with authoritarian governance, minimal state capacity, or fundamental rejection of cultural diversity as a legitimate policy concern. However, the theoretical insights may still be relevant for understanding integration processes even in contexts where policy applications are limited.

Roadmap for the Reader

The monograph is structured to build systematically from existing knowledge towards theoretical innovation and practical application. Each chapter contributes essential components to the overall argument while also standing as a significant analysis in its own right.

Chapter 2 provides the foundation for theoretical innovation by conducting a comprehensive survey of existing approaches to cultural distance in immigrant integration studies. The chapter analyses assimilationist approaches including both classical and neo-assimilation theories, examining their insights and limitations for understanding cultural distance effects. Co-existence approaches including multiculturalism and segmented assimilation theories receive detailed analysis, as do critical approaches that emphasize power relations and structural factors. Constructivist approaches that focus on the social construction of cultural boundaries are also examined. The chapter concludes by identifying common denominators across theoretical traditions and highlighting research gaps that motivate the development of the CDIM framework.

Chapter 3 analyses three major theoretical frameworks that provide essential building blocks for understanding cultural distance but have not been systematically integrated into immigration studies. Huntington's civilizational theory receives critical analysis for its insights into large-scale cultural differences and their political implications, while acknowledging the limitations and controversies surrounding this approach (Huntington, 1996). Hofstede's cultural dimensions framework is examined for its systematic approach to measuring cultural variation, despite criticisms of its methodology and assumptions (Hofstede, 2001). The Inglehart-Welzel cultural map provides insights into the relationship between cultural values and societal development that are essential for understanding integration processes (Inglehart & Welzel, 2005).

Chapter 4 presents the core Cultural Distance Integration Model through detailed analysis of its key components. The three-level architecture distinguishing surface, intermediate, and deep cultural levels provides a framework for understanding how different types of cultural differences affect integration processes. The cultural distance threshold hypothesis receives extensive development, including specification of different threshold types and the mechanisms that produce them. The analysis of mechanisms through which cultural distance affects integration covers individual psychological processes, community social dynamics, and institutional adaptation challenges. The bidirectional nature of cultural distance effects receives detailed treatment, showing how immigration affects both immigrant and host populations. Temporal dynamics and generational effects are analysed to understand how cultural distance impacts change over time. The chapter concludes with analysis of scope conditions and contextual factors that moderate cultural distance effects.

Chapter 5 provides mathematical formalizations of the theoretical framework developed in Chap. 4. The core mathematical framework establishes basic equations for measuring cultural distance and predicting integration outcomes. Mechanism-specific models provide detailed mathematical representations of individual, community, and institutional processes. The bidirectional adaptation model formalizes the mutual influence processes between immigrant and host populations. Threshold dynamics receive mathematical treatment that enables quantitative analysis of discontinuous effects. Models for generational, gender, and class variations provide tools for understanding how cultural distance effects vary across different population subgroups. The policy intervention model translates theoretical insights into quantitative tools for policy design and evaluation.

Chapter 6 positions the CDIM framework within existing theoretical traditions by showing how it relates to and extends assimilation, co-existence, critical, and constructivist approaches. Rather than rejecting previous theoretical work, this chapter demonstrates how the CDIM framework synthesizes their insights while addressing their limitations.

The analysis shows how the mathematical formalization provides tools for resolving theoretical debates and generating testable predictions. The chapter concludes with discussion of the implications of the CDIM framework for future theoretical development in immigrant integration studies.

Chapter 7 translates the theoretical framework into concrete policy implications through development of a precision integration policy architecture. The threshold-based policy framework shows how interventions can be calibrated to specific cultural distance levels for maximum effectiveness. Mechanism-specific policy interventions provide detailed guidance for addressing individual, community, and institutional integration challenges. The bidirectional adaptation and policy symmetry framework shows how policies must address both immigrant and host society populations. Contextual adaptation and dynamic policy calibration provide tools for adjusting policies to different local contexts and changing conditions. Generational policy sequencing addresses the temporal dimension of integration processes. The gender-responsive policy framework recognizes how cultural distance effects vary by gender. Resource optimization approaches provide tools for maximizing policy effectiveness within budget constraints. Implementation challenges and institutional requirements receive detailed analysis to ensure that policy recommendations are practically feasible.

Chapter 8 provides a comprehensive summary of key findings and their implications for both theoretical understanding and policy practice. The chapter discusses limitations of the current framework and identifies directions for future research that can extend and refine the CDIM approach. The conclusion emphasizes both the theoretical contributions of the work and its practical potential for improving integration outcomes in diverse societies.

References

Alba, R., & Nee, V. (2003). *Remaking the American mainstream: Assimilation and contemporary immigration*. Harvard University Press.

Alesina, A., Giuliano, P., & Nunn, N. (2013). On the origins of gender roles: Women and the plough. *Quarterly Journal of Economics, 128*(2), 469–530. https://doi.org/10.1093/qje/qjt005

Allport, G. (1954). *The nature of prejudice*. Addison-Wesley.

Bardach, E., & Patashnik, E. M. (2020). *A practical guide for policy analysis*. Sage.

Becker, G. S. (1957). *The economics of discrimination*. University of Chicago Press.

Becker, G. S. (1976). *The economic approach to human behavior*. University of Chicago Press.
Becker, G. S. (1991). *A treatise on the family* (Enlarged ed.). Harvard University Press.
Berry, J. W. (1997). Immigration, acculturation, and adaptation. *Applied sychology, 46*(1),5–34.https://doi.org/10.1111/j.1464-0597.1997.tb01087.x
Berry, J. W. (2006). Acculturation: Living successfully in two cultures. *International Journal of Intercultural Relations, 29*(6), 697–712. https://doi.org/10.1016/j.ijintrel.2005.07.013
Bhabha, H. K. (1994). *The location of culture*. Routledge.
Bloemraad, I. (2006). *Becoming a citizen: Incorporating immigrants and refugees in the United States and Canada*. University of California Press.
Borjas, G. J. (1999). *Heaven's Door*. Princeton University Press.
Borjas, G. J. (2019). Reflections on immigration economics. In B. Elsner (Ed.), *Foundations of migration economics* (pp. 573–582). Oxford University Press.
Bourdieu, P. (1986). The forms of capital. In J. Richardson (Ed.), *Handbook of theory and research for the sociology of education* (pp. 241–258). Greenwood.
Entman, R. M., & Rojecki, A. (2000). *The black image in the white mind: Media and race in America*. University of Chicago Press.
European Commission. (n.d.). *Third-country national*. Retrieved July 19, 2025, from https://home-affairs.ec.europa.eu/pages/glossary/third-country-national_en
Fixsen, D. L., Naoom, S. F., Blase, K. A., Friedman, R. M., & Wallace, F. (2005). *Implementation research: A synthesis of the literature*. University of South Florida.
Garip, F. (2008). Social capital and migration: How do similar resources lead to divergent outcomes? *Demography*, 45(3), 591–617. http://www.jstor.org/stable/25475992
Geertz, C. (1973). *The interpretation of cultures*. Basic Books.
Giles, H., Coupland, J., & Coupland, N. (1991). *Contexts of accommodation: Developments in applied sociolinguistics*. Cambridge University Press.
Goldin, C. (2021). *Career and family: Women's century-long journey toward equity*. Princeton University Press.
Gordon, M. (1964). *Assimilation in American life. The role of race, religion, and national origins*. Oxford University Press.
Granovetter, M. (1978). Threshold models of collective behavior. *American Journal of Sociology, 83*(6), 1420–1443. https://doi.org/10.1086/226707
Hall, E. T. (1976). *Beyond culture*. Anchor Books.
Hall, R. (2020). *Mixing methods in social research*. Sage.
Hofstede, G. (2001). *Culture's consequences: Comparing values, Behaviors, institutions and organizations across nations*. Sage.
Huntington, S. P. (1996). *The clash of civilizations and the remaking of world order*. Simon & Schuster.

Inglehart, R. F. (1997). *Modernization and Postmodernization: Cultural, economic, and political change in 43 societies*. Princeton University Press.
Inglehart, R. F. (2018). *Cultural evolution: People's motivations are changing, and reshaping the world*. Cambridge University Press.
Inglehart, R. F., & Welzel, C. (2005). *Modernization, cultural change, and democracy*. Cambridge University Press.
Jones, G. (2022). *The culture transplant. How migrants make the economies they move to a lot like the ones they left*. Stanford University Press.
Kindler, M., Ratcheva, V., & Piechowska, M. (2015). *Social networks, social capital and migrant integration at local level: European literature review*. IRiS Working Paper Series, No. 6/2015.
Kingston, C., & Caballero, G. (2009). Comparing theories of institutional change. *Journal of Institutional Economics, 5*(2), 151–180. https://doi.org/10.1017/S1744137409001283
Kymlicka, W. (1996). *Multicultural Citizenship*. Oxford University Press.
Kymlicka, W. (2010). The rise and fall of multiculturalism? New debates on inclusion and accommodation in diverse societies. *International Social Science Journal, 61*(199), 97–112. https://doi.org/10.1111/j.1468-2451.2010.01750.x
Lőrincz, L., & Németh, B. (2022). How social capital is related to migration between communities? *European Journal of Population, 38*(5), 1119–1143. https://doi.org/10.1007/s10680-022-09642-3
Macuchova, Z., & Rauhut, D. (2023). Measuring immigrant integration—How, what and for whom? In D. Rauhut (Ed.), *New methods and theory on immigrant integration: Insights from remote and peripheral areas* (pp. 123–141). Edward Elgar.
Macy, M. W., & Evtushenko, A. (2020). Threshold models of collective behavior II: The predictability paradox and spontaneous instigation. *Sociological Science, 7*, 628–648. https://doi.org/10.15195/v7.a26
March, J. G., & Olsen, J. P. (1986). Popular sovereignty and the search for appropriate institutions. *Journal of Public Policy, 6*(4), 341–370. https://doi.org/10.1017/S0143814X00004207
March, J. G., & Olsen, J. P. (1989). *Rediscovering institutions. The organizational basis of politics*. Free Press.
Milgrom, P., North, D., & Weingast, B. (1990). The role of institutions in the revival of trade: The law merchant, private judges and the champagne fairs. *Economics and Politics, 2*(1), 1–23. https://doi.org/10.1111/j.1468-0343.1990.tb00020.x
Miller, J. H., & Page, S. E. (2007). *Complex adaptive systems: An introduction to computational models of social life*. Princeton University Press.
Modood, T. (2007). *Multiculturalism: A Civic Idea*. Polity Press.
Mügge, L., & van der Haar, M. (2016). Who is an immigrant and who requires integration? Categorization of European policies. In B. Garcés-Mascareñas &

R. Penninx (Eds.), *Integration processes and policies in Europe* (pp. 77–90). Springer.
Musterd, S. (2005). Social and ethnic segregation in Europe: Levels, causes, and effects. *Journal of Urban Affairs, 27*(3), 331–348. https://doi.org/10.1111/j.0735-2166.2005.00239.x
Norris, P., & Inglehart, R. F. (2019). *Cultural backlash: Trump, Brexit, and authoritarian populism*. Cambridge University Press.
North, D. C. (1990). *Institutions, institutional change and economic performance*. Cambridge University Press.
North, D. C. (1991). Institutions. *Journal of Economic Perspectives, 5*(1), 97–112. https://doi.org/10.1257/jep.5.1.97
North, D. C., & Thomas, R. P. (1973). *The rise of the Western world. A new economic history*. Cambridge University Press.
OECD. (2024). *The economic case for greater LGBTI+ equality in the United States*. OECD Publishing. https://doi.org/10.1787/5adfe3a5-en
Ogbu, J. U., & Simons, H. D. (1998). Voluntary and involuntary minorities: A cultural-ecological theory of school performance with some implications for education. *Anthropology & Education Quarterly, 29*(2), 155–188. https://doi.org/10.1525/aeq.1998.29.2.155
Pager, D., & Shepherd, H. (2008). The sociology of discrimination: Racial discrimination in employment, housing, credit, and consumer markets. *Annual Review of Sociology, 34*, 181–209. https://doi.org/10.1146/annurev.soc.33.040406.131740
Park, R., & Burgess, E. (1921). *Introduction to the science of sociology*. University of Chicago Press.
Penninx, R. (2003). *Integration: The role of communities, institutions and the state*. Migration Policy Institute, October 1, 2003. Retrieved August 17, 2025, from www.migrationpolicy.org
Pettigrew, T. F. (1998). Intergroup contact theory. *Annual Review of Psychology, 49*(1), 65–85. https://doi.org/10.1146/annurev.psych.49.1.65
Pettigrew, T. F., & Tropp, L. R. (2006). A meta-analytic test of intergroup contact theory. *Journal of Personality and Social Psychology, 90*(5), 751–783. https://doi.org/10.1037/0022-3514.90.5.751
Phinney, J. S. (1990). Ethnic identity in adolescents and adults: Review of research. *Psychological Bulletin, 108*(3), 499–514. https://doi.org/10.1037/0033-2909.108.3.499
Portes, A., & Rumbaut, R. G. (2001). *Legacies: The story of the immigrant second generation*. University of California Press.
Portes, A., & Zhou, M. (1993). The new second generation: Segmented assimilation and its variants. *Annals of the American Academy of Political and Social Science, 530*(1), 74–96. https://doi.org/10.1177/0002716293530001006

Putnam, R. (2007). E pluribus unum: Diversity and community in the twenty-first century. *Scandinavian Political Studies, 30*(2), 137–174. https://doi.org/10.1111/j.1467-9477.2007.00176.x

Rauhut, D. (2020). *Integration and informal institutions. Society, 57*(2), 211–218. https://doi.org/10.1007/s12115-020-00467-6

Rosenberg, N., & Birdzell, L. E., Jr. (1986). *How the west grew rich: The economic transformation of the industrial world*. Basic Books.

Rubin, A., & Babbie, E. R. (2014). *Research methods for social work*. Brooks/Cole Cengage.

Sides, J., Tesler, M., & Vavreck, L. (2018). *Identity crisis: The 2016 presidential campaign and the Battle for the meaning of America*. Princeton University Press.

Swedberg, R. (2014). *The art of social theory*. Princeton University Press.

Tajfel, H., & Turner, J. (1979). An integrative theory of intergroup conflict. In W. G. Austin & S. Worchel (Eds.), *The social psychology of intergroup relations* (pp. 33–47). Brooks/Cole.

Thelen, E., & Smith, L. B. (1994). *A dynamic systems approach to the development of cognition and action*. MIT Press.

Wimmer, A. (2008). The making and unmaking of ethnic boundaries: A multilevel process theory. *American Journal of Sociology, 113*(4), 970–1022. https://doi.org/10.1086/522803

Witherington, D. C. (2007). The dynamic systems approach as Metatheory for Developmental Psychology. *Human Development, 50*(2–3), 127–153. https://doi.org/10.1159/000100943

CHAPTER 2

Cultural Distance in Immigrant Integration

Introduction

The relationship between informal institutions as cultural distance and immigrant integration represents one of the most contested and consequential debates in contemporary migration studies (Bisin & Verdier, 2001; Bloemraad et al., 2023). As societies worldwide struggle with increasing cultural diversity, fundamental questions persist about how cultural differences between immigrants and receiving societies should be understood, measured, and addressed through policy and practice (Berry et al., 2006; Hugo, 2005; Jones, 2022). As they shape integration programmes, citizenship requirements, and the daily experiences of millions of immigrants navigating new cultural environments, these questions are not merely academic (Dutch Government, n.d.; Slade, 2010). Yet despite decades of research and policy experimentation, scholars and practitioners remain deeply divided on whether cultural distance represents a barrier to overcome, a resource to preserve, or a social construction that obscures more fundamental structural inequalities (Brubaker, 2001; Bloemraad et al., 2023; D'Amato & Russo, 2025).

This chapter provides a comprehensive review of how different theoretical traditions have conceptualized cultural distance and its role in immigrant integration processes. By examining assimilationist, co-existence, critical, and constructivist approaches, we map the theoretical landscape that has dominated integration research while identifying

D. Rauhut, *Institutional Economics and Immigrant Integration*,
https://doi.org/10.1007/978-3-032-28361-0_2

significant gaps that limit our understanding of how cultural distance operates in practice. This review serves as the foundation for positioning the empirical contributions of this book. Understanding where current theories converge and diverge is essential for developing more nuanced frameworks that can better capture the complex realities of cultural difference in contemporary diverse societies.

Assimilationist Approaches

The assimilationist tradition conceptualizes cultural distance as a measurable gap between immigrant cultures and host societies that must be bridged for successful integration. This perspective draws heavily on classical sociological work by Robert Park and the Chicago School, who viewed assimilation as a natural, linear process whereby immigrants gradually adopt the cultural practices, values, and identities of the receiving society (Park & Burgess, 1921). Milton Gordon's influential work *Assimilation in American Life* (1964) systematized this approach by distinguishing between cultural assimilation (acculturation) and structural assimilation, arguing that cultural distance creates barriers to both processes.

Contemporary assimilationist scholars like Richard Alba and Victor Nee have refined these arguments through their 'new assimilation theory', which acknowledges that assimilation can be segmented and that outcomes vary across immigrant groups (Alba & Nee, 2003). Their empirical work demonstrates that cultural distance, particularly in terms of language, religion, and family structures, significantly predicts integration outcomes across generations. Studies using this framework consistently find that immigrants from culturally similar backgrounds (European immigrants to North America, for instance) achieve educational, economic, and social parity with native populations more rapidly than those from culturally distant societies.

Empirical research within this tradition has extensively documented how specific cultural differences affect integration trajectories. Borjas' economic analyses show that immigrants from countries with educational systems and labour market structures similar to host countries achieve better economic outcomes (Borjas, 1999). Similarly, research on language acquisition demonstrates that linguistic distance from the host country language significantly affects both speed of acquisition and ultimate proficiency levels, with cascading effects on employment and social integration (Chiswick & Miller, 2005).

The policy implications of assimilationist approaches emphasize reducing cultural distance through targeted interventions. This includes mandatory language training, civic education programmes, and cultural orientation courses designed to familiarize immigrants with host society norms and expectations. Countries like Denmark and the Netherlands have implemented comprehensive integration programmes based on these principles, requiring immigrants to demonstrate cultural knowledge and language proficiency for permanent residence and citizenship.

Co-existence Approaches

Multiculturalist approaches fundamentally reframe cultural distance from a barrier to overcome into a form of diversity to be accommodated and celebrated. This theoretical tradition emerged from the work of scholars like John Berry, whose acculturation model proposed that successful integration could occur through multiple pathways, including maintaining heritage culture while adopting aspects of the host culture (Berry, 1997). Integration occurs when individuals are able to adopt the cultural norms of the dominant or host culture while maintaining their culture of origin.

Theoretical work by Will Kymlicka has been particularly influential in articulating how liberal democratic societies can accommodate cultural distance without compromising social cohesion (Kymlicka, 1995). His arguments for group-differentiated rights suggest that cultural distance need not be eliminated but rather institutionally recognized and protected. This perspective emphasizes that successful integration requires changes from both immigrants and receiving societies, challenging the unidirectional adaptation assumed by assimilationist models.

Empirical research supporting multiculturalist approaches has documented the benefits of cultural maintenance for immigrant wellbeing and integration outcomes. Studies consistently show that immigrants who maintain strong connections to their heritage cultures while also engaging with host societies report higher levels of psychological wellbeing and demonstrate better adaptation outcomes (Phinney et al., 2001). Research on ethnic enclaves demonstrates that these culturally concentrated communities can serve as bridges rather than barriers to broader societal integration, providing social capital and economic opportunities while preserving cultural practices.

Canadian research has been particularly influential in demonstrating the viability of multiculturalist integration models. Studies of Canada's official multiculturalism policy show that high levels of cultural diversity can co-exist with strong national identification and social cohesion (Bloemraad, 2006). This research challenges assumptions that cultural distance necessarily undermines social solidarity, instead suggesting that inclusive policies can foster integration across cultural differences.

Policy applications of multiculturalist approaches emphasize accommodation rather than assimilation. This includes official recognition of multiple languages, support for cultural and religious organizations, modification of institutional practices to accommodate diverse cultural needs, and anti-discrimination legislation. Countries like Canada and Australia have implemented comprehensive multiculturalist policies based on these principles, creating frameworks for managing cultural distance through institutional accommodation rather than cultural convergence.

Within the co-existence paradigm, two important theoretical developments have emerged that offer more nuanced approaches to cultural distance: superdiversity and interculturalism. These frameworks represent sophisticated responses to the perceived limitations of traditional multiculturalism in addressing contemporary migration patterns and integration challenges.

The concept of *superdiversity*, developed by Steven Vertovec, acknowledges that contemporary societies have moved beyond simple multicultural models to encompass a diversity that goes far beyond the previous level and is highly complex. Vertovec's framework recognizes that cultural distance can no longer be understood through simple origin-destination dyads but must account for multiple, intersecting forms of difference including country of origin, migration pathway, legal status, employment patterns, spatial distribution, and transnational connections (Vertovec, 2007).

The superdiversity approach fundamentally reconceptualizes cultural distance as multidimensional and dynamic rather than static. Rather than focusing on traditional ethnic or national categories, superdiversity emphasizes how migration patterns have created complex configurations of difference that intersect and interact in unpredictable ways. This perspective suggests that cultural distance is not simply about difference between immigrant and host cultures, but about managing complexity arising from multiple, simultaneous forms of diversity.

Empirical research on superdiversity has documented how traditional approaches to measuring cultural distance fail to capture the complexity of contemporary diverse societies. Studies in cities like London, Toronto, and Amsterdam show how neighbourhoods characterized by superdiversity develop their own integration dynamics that cannot be predicted from simple cultural distance measures (Meissner & Vertovec, 2015). Research demonstrates that in superdiverse contexts, immigrants often integrate through contact with other immigrant groups rather than directly with established host populations, creating new forms of intercultural competence that transcend traditional assimilation models.

Policy implications of superdiversity approaches emphasize adaptive governance and localized responses rather than standardized integration programmes. This framework suggests that as countries become more diverse, a new framework is needed to mediate these relationships and that this will require new systems that can respond to complexity rather than attempting to reduce it. Cities implementing superdiversity-informed policies focus on creating platforms for cross-cultural interaction and developing institutional capacity to respond to unpredictable forms of diversity rather than managing predetermined cultural differences.

Interculturalism, particularly as developed by Ted Cantle and others, offers an alternative to multiculturalism that emphasizes interaction and dialogue across cultural differences rather than simply accommodating separate cultural communities. This approach treats cultural distance not as something to be preserved or eliminated, but as a starting point for productive interaction and mutual learning.

The theoretical foundations of interculturalism distinguish it from multiculturalism in several key ways. Interculturalism is understood as being less focused on distinct group identities and more oriented towards integration and blending than multiculturalism, while also placing greater emphasis on fostering unity, such as societal cohesion and national citizenship. This approach suggests that while cultural differences should be recognized and respected, the goal should be to create opportunities for meaningful interaction and mutual influence rather than parallel co-existence.

Interculturalism addresses cultural distance through an emphasis on contact and dialogue. Rather than assuming that cultural differences will naturally lead to conflict or that they should be managed through separation, intercultural approaches actively promote interaction across difference. This perspective draws on contact theory from social psychology, which suggests that meaningful contact under appropriate conditions can reduce prejudice and build understanding across group boundaries.

Empirical research supporting intercultural approaches has documented the benefits of structured intercultural contact for both immigrants and host society members. Studies of intercultural programs in cities across Europe show that participants develop more nuanced understandings of cultural difference and report greater comfort with diversity following sustained intercultural engagement (Cantle, 2012). Research on workplace intercultural training demonstrates that programs focusing on interaction skills rather than cultural knowledge produce better integration outcomes and reduced cultural conflict.

The policy applications of interculturalism emphasize creating opportunities for meaningful contact and dialogue across cultural differences. This includes intercultural mediation programs, mixed housing policies that prevent ethnic concentration, intercultural education programs that bring together students from different backgrounds, and community development initiatives that require collaboration across cultural boundaries. Supporters claim that multiculturalism has struggled to keep pace with the growing complexity and diversity of modern societies, particularly in addressing varied forms of difference and otherness, and that intercultural strategies offer more effective solutions to today's integration issues by emphasizing engagement over mere co-existence.

Critical Approaches

Critical theoretical perspectives challenge the very concept of cultural distance as potentially masking power relations, structural inequalities, and processes of racialization. Drawing from post-colonial theory, critical race theory, and neo-Marxist analyses, this tradition argues that cultural distance narratives often serve to individualize and culturalize what are fundamentally structural problems (Schinkel, 2018). Schinkel's critique of immigrant integration research argues that the field suffers from poor conceptual work and that integration monitoring and research often serves to reproduce exclusionary practices rather than facilitate genuine inclusion.

Critical scholars like Ghassan Hage argue that multiculturalism itself can be a form of 'white governance' that allows dominant groups to manage diversity while maintaining their privileged position (Hage, 1998). This perspective suggests that both assimilationist and multiculturalist approaches to cultural distance may obscure how integration processes are shaped by racism, class relations, and colonial histories rather than cultural differences per se.

Empirical research within critical frameworks has documented how cultural distance narratives often correlate with racialization processes rather than actual cultural differences. Studies show that immigrant groups from the Global South face integration barriers that cannot be explained by cultural distance alone, suggesting that racialization and structural discrimination play crucial roles (Colic-Peisker & Tilbury, 2006). Research on labour market integration demonstrates that immigrants with similar educational qualifications face differential outcomes based on their country of origin and perceived cultural distance, indicating that discrimination rather than cultural factors may drive integration outcomes.

Critical research has also examined how cultural distance discourse can serve assimilationist ends while appearing to celebrate diversity. Studies of integration programmes in European countries show how requirements for cultural adaptation are often framed in terms of gender equality or secular values, making assimilationist demands appear progressive while targeting specific immigrant communities (Bracke, 2012).

The policy implications of critical approaches emphasize structural change rather than cultural accommodation or assimilation. This includes anti-racism initiatives, employment equity programmes, addressing institutional discrimination, and recognizing how historical and ongoing colonial relations shape contemporary integration challenges. Rather than focusing on managing cultural distance, critical approaches advocate for dismantling the structural barriers that create differential integration outcomes across immigrant groups.

Constructivist Approaches

Constructivist theoretical frameworks treat cultural distance as socially constructed rather than objectively given, focusing on how cultural differences are perceived, interpreted, and negotiated through social interactions. This approach draws from symbolic interactionism, social constructionism, and ethnomethodological traditions to examine how both immigrants and host society members make sense of cultural differences in specific contexts (Brubaker, 2001).

Constructivist scholars like Rogers Brubaker argue that ethnicity and cultural difference should be understood as contingent products of social interaction rather than fixed group properties (Brubaker, 2002). This perspective emphasizes how cultural distance is actively constructed through everyday encounters, media representations, and institutional practices rather than simply reflecting pre-existing cultural differences.

Recent work by scholars like Andreas Wimmer has developed boundary-making approaches that examine how ethnic and cultural boundaries are drawn, maintained, and transformed through social processes (Wimmer, 2008). This research shows how the salience and meaning of cultural differences vary across contexts and change over time through processes of boundary crossing, blurring, and shifting.

Empirical research within constructivist frameworks has documented significant variation in how cultural distance is perceived and experienced across different contexts. Ethnographic studies show how the same cultural practices can be interpreted differently depending on the social setting, the individuals involved, and the broader political context (Levitt & Waters, 2002). Research on second-generation immigrants demonstrates how cultural distance is actively negotiated rather than simply inherited, with individuals strategically emphasizing or downplaying cultural differences depending on situational demands.

Studies of workplace integration show how cultural distance is constructed through organizational practices and interpersonal interactions rather than simply reflecting pre-existing cultural differences (Lamont & Molnar, 2002). This research demonstrates how successful integration often involves mutual adaptation and learning rather than unidirectional cultural change.

Policy implications of constructivist approaches emphasize dialogue, interaction, and mutual learning rather than either assimilation or accommodation. This includes programmes that bring together immigrants and host society members for sustained interaction, training programmes that help institutions recognize how they construct cultural boundaries, and policies that acknowledge the dynamic and contextual nature of cultural difference. Cities like Toronto and Amsterdam have experimented with dialogue-based integration programmes that reflect constructivist principles, focusing on relationship-building and mutual understanding rather than cultural convergence or preservation.

Common Denominators

Despite their theoretical differences, these approaches share several underlying commonalities. All four traditions struggle with the fundamental question of how cultural differences should be understood and managed in diverse societies, though they reach vastly different conclusions. Each approach also makes assumptions about the nature of culture itself, i.e., whether it is fixed or fluid, individual or collective, and whether cultural boundaries are meaningful or constructed.

Interestingly, all traditions acknowledge that integration is a two-way process to some degree, though they differ dramatically in where they place emphasis (Ager & Strang, 2008). Even assimilationist approaches now recognize that receiving societies must provide opportunities and access, while critical approaches focus almost entirely on structural changes needed from host societies. There is also a shared recognition across traditions that simple linear models of integration are inadequate, leading to more nuanced frameworks like segmented assimilation, superdiversity, and intersectional analyses (Portes & Zhou, 1993).

Another commonality is the increasing attention to context, whether local, national, or transnational. The superdiversity and interculturalism literatures particularly emphasize how integration processes vary dramatically across different urban contexts (Glick Schiller & Çağlar, 2009), while critical approaches highlight how colonial histories and global power relations shape contemporary integration experiences (Grosfoguel, 2004; Levitt & Glick Schiller, 2004).

Research Gaps

The overview presented in this chapter highlights several enduring and interrelated research gaps that continue to limit our understanding of cultural distance in immigrant integration. These gaps cut across theoretical traditions and persist despite rich bodies of empirical work. A key omission remains the under-theorization of gendered experiences within cultural distance frameworks. While critical approaches gesture towards how narratives of cultural distance have been used to regulate immigrant women under the guise of secular or liberal values (Anthias, 2012; Bracke, 2012), few studies offer a systematic interrogation of how patriarchal structures in both origin and destination societies intersect with cultural perceptions, or how gender relations shape the integration process itself.

Equally striking is the lack of generational analysis. Although constructivist literature briefly explores second-generation identity negotiation, the broader field seldom engages with how cultural distance is perceived, reimagined, and recalibrated across generations (Rumbaut, 2004; Orellana, 2009). The role of children as cultural brokers and the transformation of cultural boundaries through intergenerational exchange remain underexamined and warrant deeper empirical investigation.

The marginalization of class and socioeconomic stratification also presents a significant lacuna. While economic theories, notably those advanced by Borjas (1999), incorporate human capital considerations, the interplay between cultural distance and social class remains conceptually thin across most traditions. Studies have yet to fully explore how economic privilege or precarity mediate immigrants' access to cultural resources and determine whether cultural maintenance is a choice or a constraint (Erel, 2010).

Beyond individual identities, temporal and contextual dimensions of cultural distance require greater analytical attention. Although superdiversity theory introduces a more fluid and multidimensional account of difference (Vertovec, 2007; Meissner & Vertovec, 2015), the temporal evolution of cultural distance—how it shifts across life stages, policy cycles, or geopolitical climates—is rarely addressed longitudinally. Similarly, while urban diversity has stimulated policy innovation, most literature remains bound to national frameworks, limiting our understanding of how hyperlocal contexts and transnational networks co-produce integration dynamics (Glick Schiller & Çağlar, 2009).

Perhaps most significantly, intersectional analysis remains conspicuously absent across all traditions. There has been insufficient theorization of how cultural distance interacts with other axes of inequality such as race, sexuality, age, disability, and religion (Crenshaw, 1989; Anthias, 2008; Luibhéid, 2008). The tendency to treat cultural difference as a singular variable obscures the complex ways that multiple identities and systems of power shape integration experiences. As such, the apparent neutrality of cultural distance must be problematized, and future research should interrogate its epistemological foundations alongside its practical implications.

This chapter has sought to map the contours of cultural distance scholarship while identifying avenues for further exploration. To move the field forward, future studies must embrace methodological pluralism, engage with intersectionality more rigorously, and attend to the lived realities of integration beyond theoretical abstraction. Only through such nuanced and inclusive approaches can researchers begin to unravel the layered meanings and consequences of cultural distance in an increasingly diverse world.

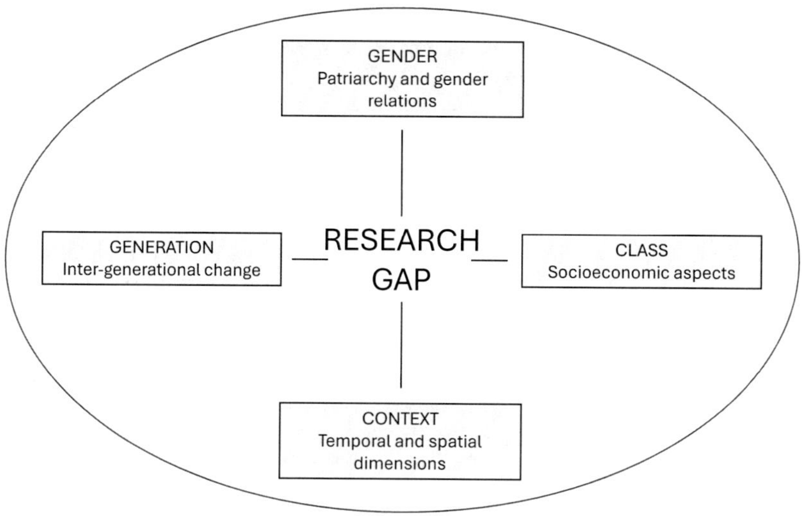

Fig. 2.1 A visualization of the research gap. Source: Own elaboration

To visually encapsulate the multidimensional gaps and theoretical silences discussed above, Fig. 2.1 offers a schematic representation of how various intersecting factors (gender, generation, class, and locality) complicate the concept of cultural distance in integration research.

References

Ager, A., & Strang, A. (2008). Understanding integration: A conceptual framework. *Journal of Refugee Studies, 21*(2), 166–191. https://doi.org/10.1093/jrs/fen016

Alba, R., & Nee, V. (2003). *Remaking the American mainstream: Assimilation and contemporary immigration*. Harvard University Press.

Anthias, F. (2008). Thinking through the lens of translocational positionality: An intersectionality frame for understanding identity and belonging. *Translocations: Migration and Social Change, 4*(1), 5–20.

Anthias, F. (2012). Intersectional what? Social divisions, intersectionality and levels of analysis. *Ethnicities, 13*(1), 3–19. https://doi.org/10.1177/1468796812463547

Berry, J. W. (1997). Immigration, acculturation, and adaptation. *Applied Psychology, 46*(1), 5–34. https://doi.org/10.1111/j.1464-0597.1997.tb01087.x

Berry, J. W., Phinney, J. S., Sam, D. L., & Vedder, P. (2006). *Immigrant youth in cultural transition: Acculturation, identity, and adaptation across national contexts.* Psychology Press.

Bisin, A., & Verdier, T. (2001). The economics of cultural transmission and the dynamics of preferences. *Journal of Economic Theory, 97*(2), 298–319. https://doi.org/10.1006/jeth.2000.2678

Bloemraad, I. (2006). *Becoming a citizen: Incorporating immigrants and refugees in the United States and Canada.* University of California Press.

Bloemraad, I., Esses, V. M., Kymlicka, W., & Zhou, Y. Y. (2023). *Unpacking immigrant integration: Concepts, mechanisms, and context.* Retrieved August 4, 2025, from https://thedocs.worldbank.org/en/doc/454db131e2fb1cd0394 09bd6f78e1778-0050062023/original/Social-integration-FINAL-FORMATTED.pdf

Borjas, G. J. (1999). *Heaven's door. Immigration policy and the American economy.* Princeton University Press.

Bracke, S. (2012). From 'saving women' to 'saving gays': Rescue narratives and their dis/continuities. *European Journal of Women's Studies, 19*(2), 237–252. https://doi.org/10.1177/1350506811435032

Brubaker, R. (2001). The return of assimilation? Changing perspectives on immigration and its sequels in France, Germany, and the United States. *Ethnic and Racial Studies, 24*(4), 531–548. https://doi.org/10.1080/014198 70120049770

Brubaker, R. (2002). Ethnicity without groups. *European Journal of Sociology, 43*(2), 163–189. https://doi.org/10.1017/S0003975602001066

Cantle, T. (2012). *Interculturalism: The new era of cohesion and diversity.* Palgrave Macmillan.

Chiswick, B. R., & Miller, P. W. (2005). Linguistic distance: A quantitative measure of the distance between English and other languages. *Journal of Multilingual and Multicultural Development, 26*(1), 1–11. https://doi.org/1 0.1080/14790710508668395

Colic-Peisker, V., & Tilbury, F. (2006). Employment niches for recent refugees: Segmented labour market in twenty-first century Australia. *Journal of Refugee Studies, 19*(2), 203–229. https://doi.org/10.1093/jrs/fej016

Crenshaw, K. W. (1989). Demarginalizing the intersection of race and sex: A black feminist critique of antidiscrimination doctrine, feminist theory and antiracist politics. *University of Chicago Legal Forum, 1989*(1), 139–167.

D'Amato, M., & Russo, F. F. (2025). Cultural doorways in the barriers to development. *The Journal of Economic Growth, 31*, 125–178. https://doi.org/10.1007/s10887-025-09253-7

Dutch Government. (n.d.). *Civic integration in the Netherlands.* Retrieved August 4, 2025, from https://www.government.nl/topics/integration-in-the-netherlands/civic-integration-in-the-netherlands

Erel, U. (2010). Migrating cultural capital: Bourdieu in migration studies. *Sociology, 44*(4), 642–660. https://doi.org/10.1177/0038038510369363

Glick Schiller, N., & Çağlar, A. (2009). Towards a comparative theory of locality in migration studies: Migrant incorporation and city scale. *Journal of Ethnic and Migration Studies, 35*(2), 177–202. https://doi.org/10.1080/13691830802586179

Gordon, M. (1964). *Assimilation in American life. The role of race, religion, and national origins.* Oxford University Press.

Grosfoguel, R. (2004). Race and ethnicity or racialized ethnicities? Identities within global coloniality. *Ethnicities, 4*(3), 315–336. https://doi.org/10.1177/1468796804045237

Hage, G. (Ed.). (1998). *White nation: Fantasies of white supremacy in a multicultural society.* Routledge.

Hugo, G. (2005). *Migrants in society: Diversity and cohesion.* International Organization for Migration. Retrieved August 4, 2025, from https://www.iom.int/sites/g/files/tmzbdl2616/files/2018-07/TP6.pdf

Jones, G. (2022). *The culture transplant. How migrants make the economies they move to a lot like the ones they left.* Stanford University Press.

Kymlicka, W. (1995). *Multicultural Citizenship.* Oxford University Press.

Lamont, M., & Molnar, V. (2002). The study of boundaries in the social sciences. *Annual Review of Sociology, 28*(1), 167–195. https://doi.org/10.1146/annurev.soc.28.110601.141107

Levitt, P., & Glick Schiller, N. (2004). Conceptualizing simultaneity: A transnational social field perspective on society. *International Migration Review, 38*(3), 1002–1039. https://doi.org/10.1111/j.1747-7379.2004.tb00227.x

Levitt, P., & Waters, M. C. (2002). *The changing face of home: The transnational lives of the second generation.* Russell Sage Foundation.

Luibhéid, E. (2008). Queer/migration: An unruly body of scholarship. *GLQ: A Journal of Lesbian and Gay Studies, 14*(2–3), 169–190. https://doi.org/10.1215/10642684-2007-029

Meissner, F., & Vertovec, S. (2015). Comparing super-diversity. *Ethnic and Racial Studies, 38*(4), 541–555. https://doi.org/10.1080/01419870.2015.980295

Orellana, M. F. (2009). *Translating childhoods: Immigrant youth, language, and culture.* Rutgers University Press.

Park, R., & Burgess, E. (1921). *Introduction to the science of sociology.* University of Chicago Press.

Phinney, J. S., Horenczyk, G., Liebkind, K., & Vedder, P. (2001). Ethnic identity, immigration, and well-being: An interactional perspective. *Journal of Social Issues, 57*(3), 493–510. https://doi.org/10.1111/0022-4537.00225

Portes, A., & Zhou, M. (1993). The new second generation: Segmented assimilation and its variants. *Annals of the American Academy of Political and Social Science, 530*(1), 74–96. https://doi.org/10.1177/0002716293530001006

Rumbaut, R. G. (2004). Ages, life stages, and generational cohorts: Decomposing the immigrant first and second generations in the United States. *International Migration Review, 38*(3), 1160–1205. https://doi.org/10.1111/j.1747-7379.2004.tb00232.x

Schinkel, W. (2018). Against 'immigrant integration': For an end to neocolonial knowledge production. *Comparative Migration Studies, 6*, 31. https://doi.org/10.1186/s40878-018-0095-1

Slade, C. (2010). Civic integration in The Netherlands. In C. Slade & M. Möllering (Eds.), *From migrant to citizen. Language and globalization* (pp. 125–144). Palgrave Macmillan.

Vertovec, S. (2007). Super-diversity and its implications. *Ethnic and Racial Studies, 30*(6), 1024–1054. https://doi.org/10.1080/01419870701599465

Wimmer, A. (2008). The making and unmaking of ethnic boundaries: A multilevel process theory. *American Journal of Sociology, 113*(4), 970–1022. https://doi.org/10.1086/522803

CHAPTER 3

Theoretical Frameworks Analysis

Institutional Economics and Informal Institutions

The analysis in this book takes as its point of departure informal institutions and their impact on immigrant integration. The relationship between cultural differences and immigrant integration can be understood through the lens of institutional economics, which provides a robust theoretical framework for analysing how informal institutions shape economic behaviour and social outcomes. This perspective reveals important connections between cultural distance, institutional theory, and integration processes that merit careful examination. Culture, as an informal institution, requires careful definition; otherwise, it becomes difficult to analyse the impact on integration processes when immigrants and natives display significant cultural differences. We need not merely acknowledge the existence of cultural difference, which can be assumed to exist even between neighbouring countries, but rather to identify when cultural difference becomes too substantial to overcome.

The legitimacy of institutions rests upon collective recognition and endorsement of particular rules and their functions within a given community. Constitutive rules, unlike their regulative counterparts that merely govern pre-existing behaviours, generate institutional realities by establishing deontic powers (encompassing rights, obligations, and permissions) that extend human agency beyond mere physical capacity and thereby construct social order (Searle, 2005). North (1991) delineated institutional

D. Rauhut, *Institutional Economics and Immigrant Integration*,
https://doi.org/10.1007/978-3-032-28361-0_3

structures into two categories: formal institutions, encompassing legislation and regulatory frameworks, and informal institutions, which comprise the normative structures, belief systems, cultural practices, and social conventions shaping human conduct. The latter category determines acceptable social interaction, prescribes appropriate behavioural codes, and perpetuates customs and traditions within communities (Milgrom et al., 1990; March & Olsen, 1986). Built on the framework by March and Olsen (1989), North (1990, p. 40) argues that informal institutions encompass behavioural norms, conventions, and conduct codes, alongside adaptations and refinements of formal regulations, constituting 'a part of the heritage that we call culture'. Cultural distance, therefore, quantifies the degree of divergence between these informal institutional structures across different societies or communities (Kingston & Caballero, 2009).

In the context of migrant communities and receiving societies, cultural distance signifies disparities in entrenched social conventions, axiological frameworks, and behavioural standards, which subsequently influence integration trajectories (Penninx, 2003). Religious frameworks constitute a significant dimension of this divergence; Western economic advancement has been attributed to the separation of religious authority from political and economic governance (Rosenberg & Birdzell Jr, 1986), as well as the emergence of centralized state authority and systematic legal codification (North & Thomas, 1973). The emphasis on individual autonomy, gender equality, and LGBTQ+ rights (Goldin, 2021; Alesina et al., 2013; OECD, 2024) is also a typical Western value.

These informal institutional frameworks significantly shape integration outcomes across various domains. Integration encompasses not simply bureaucratic or juridical accommodation, but profound adjustments to divergent modes of organizing social and economic existence. Informal institutions influence migrants' labour market participation, social network formation, trust-building processes, and engagement with both regulated and unregulated economic spheres (Rauhut, 2020). Where cultural distance is pronounced, indicating substantial divergence between origin and destination informal institutions, integration presents greater difficulties and generally necessitates extended timeframes (Jones, 2022). This complexity arises because migrants must simultaneously comprehend, accommodate, or reconcile conflicting informal normative frameworks whilst satisfying formal institutional requirements. Importantly, successful integration also demands adaptive responses from the receiving society and its established population (Rauhut, 2026b).

The connection between institutional economics and cultural distance emerges precisely through their shared foundation in informal institutions. Institutional economists have long recognized that economic behaviour cannot be explained solely through formal rules and market mechanisms (Williamson, 2000). Rather, informal constraints significantly shape how individuals and groups respond to economic incentives, form contracts, build reputations, and engage in cooperative behaviour. Cultural norms and values determine patterns of trust, reciprocity, and social cooperation that are essential for economic functioning (Guiso et al., 2006). Therefore, cultural distance represents differences in the informal institutional environment that fundamentally influences economic decision-making processes, business practices, and social coordination mechanisms.

Theoretically, integration has important implications for understanding immigrant economic integration. Differences in informal institutions between origin and destination countries can create friction in labour market participation, entrepreneurship patterns, and economic network formation (North, 1990). Immigrants from culturally distant societies may face greater challenges in signalling trustworthiness, understanding implicit business practices, or accessing social capital networks that facilitate economic advancement (see Stark, 1991). Conversely, host societies may exhibit varying degrees of institutional flexibility in accommodating different cultural practices within their economic frameworks (Williamson, 2000).

This discussion on what informal institutions as culture mean is clear, but it may still be abstract and theoretical. However, some simple examples of the practical implications of the impact informal institutions as cultural distance has on immigrant integration will illuminate their importance:

- *Individual autonomy* vs *collective obligation* (Western Europe vs. East Asia). In Scandinavian countries and much of Western Europe, individual choice in career, marriage, and lifestyle is considered a fundamental right, with adult children expected to become independent. In contrast, countries like Japan, South Korea, and China emphasize familial duty and collective decision-making, where major life choices often involve extensive family consultation and where adult children may be expected to care for elderly parents as a primary responsibility (Hofstede, 2001; Triandis, 2018; Markus & Kitayama, 1991).

- *Direct* vs. *indirect communication* (Netherlands/Germany vs. Japan/Thailand). Dutch and German cultures value direct, explicit communication where disagreement is expressed openly and considered healthy. Conversely, Japanese and Thai cultures prioritize indirect communication, face-saving, and harmony preservation, where direct contradiction or refusal is considered rude and disagreement is often expressed through subtle cues or silence (Hall, 1976; Ting-Toomey, 1988; Gudykunst & Ting-Toomey, 1988).
- *Time orientation* (Northern Europe vs. Middle East/Latin America). Germanic and Scandinavian cultures exhibit strict punctuality and monochronic time management, where schedules are rigid and lateness is disrespectful. Meanwhile, many Middle Eastern and Latin American cultures follow polychronic time orientation, where relationships take precedence over schedules, flexibility is valued, and punctuality is interpreted more loosely (Hall, 1983; Levine, 1997).
- *Gender roles and public space* (Scandinavia vs. Saudi Arabia/Afghanistan). Scandinavian countries demonstrate high gender egalitarianism with mixed-gender public spaces, equal workforce participation, and shared domestic responsibilities. This contrasts sharply with conservative interpretations in Saudi Arabia or Afghanistan, where gender segregation in public spaces has been enforced, women's mobility restricted, and traditional gender divisions strictly maintained (Hofstede, 2001; World Bank, 2012; Inglehart & Norris, 2003).
- *Trust and corruption tolerance* (Nordic countries vs. parts of Southern Europe/Asia). Nordic societies exhibit high institutional trust and zero-tolerance attitudes towards corruption, with informal norms strongly condemning nepotism or favouritism. In contrast, some Mediterranean, African, and Asian societies operate with lower institutional trust and higher acceptance of informal networks, where patronage relationships and family connections in business or government appointments are normalized and even expected (Rothstein & Stolle, 2008, Uslaner, 2002; Transparency International, 2020).
- *Alcohol and social interaction* (UK/Germany vs. Muslim-majority countries). British and German pub culture integrates alcohol consumption into normal social bonding and business networking. This directly contradicts Islamic cultural norms in countries like Iran, Saudi Arabia, or Pakistan, where alcohol consumption is religiously

prohibited and socially stigmatized (Michalak & Trocki, 2006; Room & Mäkelä, 2000).

- *Attitudes towards authority* (Australia/USA vs. Japan/South Korea). Australian and American cultures encourage questioning authority, informality with superiors, and meritocratic challenge to established hierarchies. Japanese and Korean cultures maintain strict hierarchical respect, formal language registers based on status, and deference to seniority regardless of merit (Hofstede, 2001; House et al., 2004).

The institutional economics perspective thus provides valuable insights into why cultural distance matters for integration outcomes and how policy interventions might address integration challenges. By recognizing that culture operates through informal institutions that shape economic behaviour, in this case immigrant integration, researchers and policymakers can better understand the mechanisms through which cultural differences influence immigrant experiences and develop more effective approaches to facilitating successful integration processes.

The Silent Conflict: Norms, Preferences, and Institutional Fracture

A crucial question is what happens when norms, values, and preferences, i.e., informal institutions, between different groups of the population are diametral? 'Consider, for instance, a person who favours a secularized society where gender equality and equal rights for sexual minorities are viewed as natural. They believe the individual is the most important unit in society, with rights being individual, and regard democracy as fundamental. Conversely, another person advocates for religion to guide all aspects of society, where women are subordinate to men and homosexuality is deemed a mortal sin. In this view, the clan is the most important unit in society, the individual has no rights, and autocracy is considered the best form of governance' (Rauhut, 2026a, p. 20). At a certain point, the differences in norms, values, and preferences risk being so significant that the two groups will stop interacting with each other (Rauhut & Laine, 2023). There is no open or direct conflict, but a latent one (Galtung, 1969). Still, there is a conflict; within one society there must be one moral standard. If there are several conflicting moral standards, it will be difficult to enforce judicial and moral judgement as well as to govern such a society (Lackey, 1989).

When fundamentally incompatible norms exist between different social groups, a phenomenon known as value dissonance (Lazić & Pešić, 2024), it functions as an understated yet powerful influence on modern integration processes. This contrasts with prejudice and discrimination, which are explicit and easily recognized; value dissonance remains largely implicit, woven into the psychological dimensions of social interaction (Gavrilets, 2021). It emerges through everyday activities, personal exchanges, and societal expectations, influencing how people interpret their social surroundings and navigate cultural diversity (Basic & Yakhlef, 2025; Gelfand et al., 2024). Contemporary integration frameworks typically emphasize institutional access and symbolic acknowledgement (Creary et al., 2015; Shore et al., 2018), yet they often fail to address the psychological and systemic impacts of ongoing normative tensions. These unaddressed conflicts can trigger emotional distress, erode interpersonal trust, and contribute to social division (Kelman, 2008; Ede & Starrin, 2014). There is a risk that too large cultural differences, i.e., too large differences in the factors determining informal institutions such as norms, values, and preferences, will lead to conflicts and value dissonance in society. Such development leads to a fragmentation of the society in question, which is the opposite of integration.

Traditional integration research has predominantly focused on structural factors such as education, employment, housing, and language acquisition, treating cultural differences as peripheral or easily overcome obstacles (Ager & Strang, 2008). However, there is empirical evidence suggesting that integration processes cannot be fully understood without examining the deeper cultural dimensions that shape how immigrants and host societies interact, negotiate differences, and establish mutual understanding (Schwartz et al., 2010; Rauhut, 2020).

The Imperative of Cultural Distance in Integration Research

Cultural distance theories offer a crucial analytical framework for understanding why some immigrant groups appear to integrate more readily than others, even when controlling for socioeconomic characteristics, institutional support, and length of residence. The central premise underlying these theories is that culture functions as a set of informal institutions that structure social interaction, shape behavioural expectations, and provide cognitive frameworks for interpreting social reality (North, 1990; Rauhut, 2020). When immigrants and host populations operate from fundamentally different cultural frameworks, the 'humanly devised constraints that shape human interaction' create systematic barriers to mutual understanding and social integration.

The theoretical significance of cultural distance extends beyond simple acknowledgement of cultural diversity. As Rauhut (2020) demonstrates, informal institutions can explain why integration takes place, and why some nationalities integrate into a new country, while others do not. Cultural frameworks function as deeply embedded systems of meaning-making that influence everything from family structures and authority relationships to conceptions of individual rights, gender roles, and the proper relationship between private belief and public life. These informal institutional differences create what might be termed 'integration friction', i.e., the degree of effort required to establish functional social relationships and participate effectively in host society institutions.

Recent research has demonstrated that negative responses towards migrants seem to emerge when migrants are perceived as culturally different, suggesting that cultural distance affects not only immigrant adaptation but also host society receptivity. This bidirectional dynamic underscores the importance of theoretical frameworks that can systematically analyse cultural differences and predict their likely impact on integration processes.

The theoretical frameworks examined in this chapter—Huntington's civilizational theory, Hofstede's cultural dimensions, and the Inglehart-Welzel cultural map—represent the most sophisticated attempts to conceptualize and measure cultural distance in ways that generate testable hypotheses about integration outcomes. These theories share several important characteristics that make them particularly valuable for integration research. First, they move beyond descriptive accounts of cultural differences to propose systematic frameworks for measuring and comparing cultural orientations across societies. Second, they identify fundamental dimensions of cultural variation that have direct implications for social interaction and institutional participation. Third, they offer theoretical predictions about how cultural distance should affect various aspects of the integration process.

The selection of these particular theories reflects their complementary strengths in capturing different aspects of cultural distance. Huntington's civilizational framework identifies the deepest level of cultural difference, i.e., fundamental worldview orientations that transcend national boundaries and persist across generations. Hofstede's cultural dimensions provide precise, measurable constructs that can be operationalized in empirical research and have demonstrated relevance for cross-cultural interaction in organizational and social settings. The Inglehart-Welzel framework offers the most comprehensive empirical mapping of global cultural variation, based on extensive survey data, and incorporates theoretical predictions about cultural change over time.

These theoretical frameworks are essential for advancing integration research beyond its current limitations. Contemporary integration studies often treat cultural differences as unmeasurable 'black box' factors or reduce complex cultural phenomena to simple categorical variables such as religion or region of origin. Cultural distance theories provide the analytical tools necessary to disaggregate these crude measures into specific, theoretically grounded dimensions that can be systematically analysed and compared.

Furthermore, these theories address a critical gap in integration research by explaining why integration challenges often persist across generations and resist purely structural interventions. If integration difficulties were primarily the result of language barriers, educational deficits, or economic disadvantages, we would expect these problems to diminish substantially as immigrants acquire host society skills and resources. However, persistent integration gaps in subsequent generations suggest that deeper cultural-institutional factors are at work (Alba & Nee, 2003). Cultural distance theories provide frameworks for understanding these persistent patterns by identifying the informal institutional differences that continue to shape social interaction patterns even after formal barriers have been overcome.

Huntington's Civilizational Theory: The Clash of Worldviews

Samuel Huntington (1996) provides a macro-level framework for understanding cultural differences that transcend national boundaries. He argues that in the post-Cold War era, the fundamental sources of conflict will be cultural rather than ideological or economic, occurring along the fault lines between major civilizations. His theory offers crucial insights into the deepest level of cultural distance, namely civilizational differences that shape fundamental worldviews, religious orientations, and social organization principles.

Huntington identifies eight major civilizations: Western, Confucian, Japanese, Islamic, Hindu, Slavic-Orthodox, Latin American, and African. Each civilization is characterized by distinct patterns of thought, belief systems, social structures, and cultural practices that have evolved over centuries or millennia. According to Huntington's framework, civilizations differ in their core assumptions about the relationship between God and humanity, the individual and the group, citizen and state, parents and children, and husband and wife (Huntington, 1996).

Theoretical Strengths and Applications

The primary strength of Huntington's civilizational framework lies in its recognition that cultural differences operate at multiple levels of abstraction, with civilizational differences representing the most fundamental level. Unlike theories that focus on surface-level cultural practices or national characteristics, Huntington's approach identifies deep structural differences in worldview that persist across centuries and resist easy modification through contact or education.

The framework's macro-historical perspective provides valuable insights into why certain cultural conflicts appear intractable and why integration challenges sometimes intensify rather than diminish over time. By identifying civilizational identity as a primary source of group solidarity and loyalty, the theory helps explain phenomena such as ethnic enclave formation, resistance to host society institutions, and intergenerational transmission of cultural distinctiveness.

Huntington's concept of the 'kin-country syndrome' offers particularly valuable theoretical insights for integration research. The tendency for individuals to maintain psychological and cultural connections to their civilizational homeland, regardless of citizenship or residence, suggests that successful integration may require more than individual adaptation; it may require fundamental shifts in civilizational identity and loyalty patterns.

Critical Limitations and Scholarly Debates

Despite its influential contributions, Huntington's civilizational theory faces substantial theoretical and empirical criticisms that limit its direct application to integration research. The most fundamental criticism concerns the theory's tendency towards cultural essentialism and determinism. Critics argue that Huntington's civilizational categories are overly rigid and homogeneous, failing to account for significant internal diversity within civilizations (Said, 2001; Sen, 2006). Contemporary Islamic societies, e.g., exhibit enormous variation in political systems, social practices, and cultural orientations that cannot be captured by a single civilizational designation.

The theory's emphasis on conflict and incompatibility has been criticized for underestimating the adaptive capacity of both individuals and cultures. Scholars such as Appadurai (1996) and Bhabha (1994) have demonstrated that cultural contact typically produces hybrid forms and creative adaptations rather than simple conflict or assimilation. Huntington's framework provides little theoretical space for examining how civilizational differences might be bridged, negotiated, or transformed through interaction.

Furthermore, the framework's static conception of civilizational identity conflicts with substantial evidence of cultural change and adaptation within immigrant populations. Research on second- and third-generation immigrants consistently demonstrates significant cultural adaptation and hybrid identity formation that cannot be explained by civilizational persistence theories (Portes & Rumbaut, 2001).

The theory's predictive capacity has also been questioned by empirical research demonstrating successful integration across civilizational boundaries. Studies of Asian immigration to Western countries, e.g., often show high levels of educational achievement, economic mobility, and civic participation despite substantial civilizational differences (Zhou & Bankston, 1998).

Despite these limitations, Huntington's civilizational framework remains valuable for integration theory because it identifies the deepest level of cultural difference and provides insights into why some cultural conflicts appear particularly resistant to resolution. The framework's contribution lies not in its specific predictions about civilizational conflict, but in its demonstration that cultural differences operate at multiple levels of abstraction and that the deepest differences may require generational timeframes for resolution.

Hofstede's Cultural Dimensions: Mapping Value Orientations

Geert Hofstede's cultural dimensions theory offers a more precise and measurable approach to understanding cultural differences that affect social interaction and organizational behaviour. Based initially on extensive survey research within IBM subsidiaries across multiple countries, Hofstede identified six fundamental dimensions along which national cultures vary: Power Distance, Individualism vs. Collectivism, Masculinity vs. Femininity, Uncertainty Avoidance, Long-Term vs. Short-Term Orientation, and Indulgence vs. Restraint (Hofstede, 2001; Hofstede et al., 2010).

Theoretical Strengths and Empirical Applications

The primary strength of Hofstede's framework lies in its operationalization of cultural differences into measurable dimensions that can be quantified and compared across societies. This quantitative approach enables systematic empirical research on cultural distance effects and allows for the development of testable hypotheses about integration outcomes. Recent studies have successfully used measures from Hofstede (2001) and Inglehart and Welzel (2005) to investigate economic disparities between immigrants and native populations, exploring the influence of cultural distance on income, homeownership, and poverty status.

The framework's focus on value orientations rather than surface-level cultural practices provides insights into the underlying psychological and social processes that drive integration challenges. The Power Distance Index, e.g., directly addresses fundamental differences in authority relationships and hierarchical expectations that affect educational, workplace, and political integration across multiple domains.

The multidimensional nature of Hofstede's framework allows for nuanced analysis of cultural distance that recognizes that societies may be similar on some dimensions while differing substantially on others. This complexity enables more sophisticated theoretical predictions about which types of cultural differences are most likely to create integration challenges and under what circumstances.

The framework's extensive empirical validation across multiple contexts and its widespread adoption in cross-cultural research provide a substantial foundation for integration studies. The availability of country-level scores for all dimensions enables comparative research designs and meta-analytical approaches that can identify systematic patterns across different immigration contexts.

Critical Assessments and Methodological Concerns

Despite its widespread influence, Hofstede's cultural dimensions theory faces significant methodological and theoretical criticisms that must be addressed in integration research applications. Hofstede's model has been extensively criticized for its validity and limitations, with critics like McSweeney (2002) challenging its comprehensive framework of national cultures' values, and Ailon (2008) finding inconsistencies at both theoretical and methodological levels.

The most fundamental criticism concerns the theory's reliance on national-level cultural generalizations. Critics argue that contemporary societies, particularly immigrant-receiving countries, exhibit substantial internal cultural diversity that cannot be captured by single national scores. Individual immigrants may not conform to their country's cultural profile, and host societies contain multiple subcultures with varying cultural orientations.

The framework's origins in corporate survey research have been criticized as limiting its applicability to broader social and political integration processes. The IBM survey context may have systematically excluded certain populations and cultural perspectives, potentially biasing the resulting cultural dimensions towards business-relevant values rather than broader social orientations.

Temporal stability represents another significant concern. The original surveys were conducted decades ago, and critics question whether cultural dimension scores remain valid given substantial social changes in many societies. This concern is particularly relevant for integration research, which often examines contemporary immigration flows from societies that may have experienced significant cultural change since the original measurements.

The framework's Western theoretical foundations have been criticized for imposing culturally specific conceptual categories on non-Western societies. The individualism-collectivism dimension, e.g., may not adequately capture indigenous cultural orientations that do not conform to this particular conceptual dichotomy.

Despite these limitations, Hofstede's framework continues to provide valuable insights for integration research when applied with appropriate methodological cautions. The framework's strength lies in its systematic identification of value orientations that have demonstrated relevance for cross-cultural interaction and its provision of quantitative measures that enable empirical testing of cultural distance hypotheses.

Inglehart-Welzel Cultural Map: Values in Societal Development

The Inglehart-Welzel cultural map represents the most empirically grounded approach to mapping global cultural variation, based on data from the World Values Survey covering over 100 societies. The map depicts cultural values along two fundamental dimensions: Traditional vs. Secular-Rational values (vertical axis) and Survival vs. Self-Expression values (horizontal axis) (Inglehart & Welzel, 2005).

Theoretical Innovations and Empirical Foundations

The Inglehart-Welzel framework's primary theoretical innovation lies in its integration of cultural measurement with theories of societal development and modernization. Unlike static cultural typologies, this framework incorporates theoretical predictions about cultural change over time, suggesting that economic development and generational replacement gradually move societies from traditional survival orientations towards secular-rational self-expression orientations.

The framework's empirical foundation in the World Values Survey provides unparalleled cross-national coverage and temporal depth, enabling analysis of cultural change patterns over multiple decades. This longitudinal dimension is particularly valuable for integration research because it enables analysis of how cultural distances may change over time and how different immigrant generations may experience varying degrees of cultural distance from host societies.

The framework's identification of distinct cultural clusters that correspond roughly to civilizational and regional boundaries provides empirical validation for broader theoretical arguments about deep cultural differences. The mapping reveals that Protestant Europe, Catholic Europe, English-speaking countries, Confucian societies, Islamic societies,

Orthodox societies, African societies, and Latin American societies form relatively coherent clusters on the cultural map, supporting arguments about systematic cultural patterns that transcend national boundaries.

The dynamic aspect of the framework offers crucial insights for integration theory by suggesting that cultural distance may change over generational timeframes. First-generation immigrants may maintain strong traditional survival orientations even when settling in secular-rational self-expression societies, creating maximum cultural distance. However, second and subsequent generations, socialized in the host society context, should gradually shift towards host society value orientations, reducing cultural distance over time.

Theoretical Limitations and Contemporary Challenges

Despite its empirical sophistication, the Inglehart-Welzel framework faces several theoretical limitations that affect its application to integration research. The emphasis on linear cultural change from traditional to modern may oversimplify complex cultural dynamics that include cyclical patterns, cultural revivals, and hybrid forms. Recent global trends towards religious fundamentalism, nationalist revivals, and traditional value reassertion challenge the framework's assumptions about unidirectional cultural modernization.

The framework's focus on national-level cultural patterns may obscure significant within-country variation, particularly in culturally diverse societies. This limitation is especially problematic for integration research, as immigrant populations may originate from particular regions or subcultures within their countries of origin that differ substantially from national averages.

The framework's theoretical foundations in modernization theory have been criticized for reproducing Western-centric assumptions about cultural development and progress. Critics argue that the characterization of traditional values as less developed than secular-rational values reflects cultural bias rather than objective analysis of cultural systems.

Contemporary research has also questioned whether the framework adequately captures emerging cultural orientations associated with globalization, technological change, and postmodern cultural developments. New forms of cultural expression and identity formation may not fit neatly into the traditional-secular and survival-self-expression dimensions.

Despite these limitations, the Inglehart-Welzel framework provides the most comprehensive empirical foundation for understanding global cultural variation and offers valuable insights into the relationship between cultural values and societal development. The framework's strength lies in its demonstration that cultural differences follow systematic patterns that can be measured and compared across societies, providing a foundation for theoretical predictions about integration dynamics.

The framework's incorporation of temporal change processes offers crucial insights for integration theory by suggesting that successful integration may require not just individual adaptation but generational cultural change processes. This implies that integration success should be evaluated across generational timeframes rather than within single immigrant generations, and that host society patience and long-term perspective are necessary for successful integration of culturally distant populations.

Becker's Economic Approach: Rational Choice and Social Integration

Gary Becker's pioneering application of economic analysis to social phenomena provides a fundamentally different theoretical lens for understanding immigrant integration processes. Through his seminal works *The Economics of Discrimination* (1957), *The Economic Approach to Human Behavior* (1976), and *A Treatise on the Family* (1991), Becker developed a comprehensive framework that treats integration as the outcome of rational decision-making processes by both immigrants and host society members, operating within market-like social environments where individuals maximize utility subject to constraints (Becker, 1957, 1976, 1991).

Becker's economic approach to integration rests on several core theoretical assumptions that distinguish it from cultural distance theories. First, individuals are assumed to be rational actors who make consistent choices to maximize their utility given available information and constraints. Second, social phenomena, including discrimination, family formation, and community participation, can be understood as market processes where individuals exchange resources, services, and social goods. Third, integration outcomes reflect the aggregated consequences of individual rational choices rather than cultural incompatibilities or institutional barriers per se.

Theoretical Contributions to Integration Analysis

The most significant contribution of Becker's framework to integration theory lies in its systematic analysis of discrimination as an economic phenomenon with predictable market dynamics. In *The Economics of Discrimination*, Becker reconceptualized prejudice as a preference that individuals are willing to pay to maintain, similar to any other consumption preference (Becker, 1957). Discriminators behave as if they face higher costs when interacting with members of minority groups, leading to market segregation and differential outcomes even in the absence of productivity differences.

This theoretical insight provides crucial predictions about integration dynamics that differ substantially from cultural distance explanations. According to Becker's model, discrimination should be unstable in competitive markets because non-discriminating employers gain competitive advantages by hiring qualified minority workers at below-market wages (Arrow, 1973; Darity Jr. & Mason, 1998). Over time, competitive pressures should erode discriminatory practices and promote integration through market mechanisms rather than cultural adaptation processes.

The framework's emphasis on human capital formation offers particularly valuable insights for understanding integration trajectories across generations. Becker's analysis suggests that integration success depends primarily on immigrants' and their descendants' investments in education, language acquisition, and other forms of human capital that increase productivity in host society labour markets (Becker, 1964, 1993; Chiswick, 1978; Borjas, 1999). Cultural factors matter only insofar as they affect human capital investment decisions or create market barriers to utilizing existing human capital.

Becker's analysis of family economics provides additional theoretical insights into integration processes by examining how family structures and decision-making patterns affect resource allocation, human capital investment, and intergenerational transmission (Becker, 1991). His framework predicts that family forms that maximize collective welfare through specialized role allocation and efficient resource pooling will be more successful in achieving integration outcomes, regardless of their cultural origins.

Empirical Applications and Testable Hypotheses

The strength of Becker's economic approach lies in its generation of precise, testable hypotheses about integration outcomes that can be evaluated using standard economic methodology. The framework predicts that integration success should correlate strongly with human capital characteristics, market competitiveness, and the economic returns to discrimination rather than cultural distance measures.

Recent empirical applications of Beckerian analysis to immigration have demonstrated the framework's explanatory power for understanding labour market integration, residential patterns, and intergenerational mobility. Studies utilizing human capital variables consistently find that education, language skills, and work experience explain substantial portions of immigrant-native earnings gaps, supporting Becker's emphasis on productive characteristics over cultural factors (Chiswick & Miller, 2002; Card, 2005; Dustmann & Preston, 2007).

The framework's predictions about discrimination dynamics have received mixed empirical support. While competitive market pressures do appear to reduce some forms of employment discrimination over time, persistent wage gaps and occupational segregation suggest that discriminatory preferences may be more stable than Becker's original model predicted (Charles & Guryan, 2008; Lang & Lehmann, 2012). This has led to theoretical refinements incorporating statistical discrimination, network effects, and institutional barriers that modify pure market dynamics (Phelps, 1972; Arrow, 1973; Aigner & Cain, 1977).

Becker's family economics framework has generated extensive research on immigrant family strategies, fertility decisions, and intergenerational resource transfers. Empirical studies generally support the framework's predictions about specialization and resource allocation, while revealing cultural variations in family decision-making patterns that affect integration trajectories in ways not fully captured by pure economic logic (Fernández & Fogli, 2006; Blau et al., 2013).

Critical Limitations and Theoretical Debates

Despite its analytical rigour and empirical applications, Becker's economic approach faces substantial criticisms that limit its comprehensiveness as an integration theory. The most fundamental criticism concerns the framework's methodological individualism and its reduction of complex social phenomena to individual rational choice (Coleman, 1990; Granovetter, 1985). Critics argue that integration processes involve collective identities, social movements, and institutional dynamics that cannot be adequately captured by aggregating individual utility maximization decisions.

The framework's assumption of stable, well-defined preferences has been particularly challenged by research demonstrating that cultural contact and integration experiences systematically alter individual preferences, identity formations, and decision-making frameworks (Akerlof & Kranton, 2000; Bisin & Verdier, 2001). The endogenous preference formation that occurs during integration processes violates core assumptions of Becker's static utility maximization model.

Cultural sociologists and anthropologists have criticized the framework's treatment of culture as merely another constraint or preference rather than as a constitutive element of individual identity and social interaction (Lamont & Molnar, 2002). This reductionist approach may systematically underestimate the role of meaning-making, symbolic boundaries, and collective identity formation in integration processes.

The framework's market-oriented assumptions may be particularly problematic for understanding integration in non-market contexts such as civic participation, religious communities, and informal social networks. These domains involve forms of social exchange and relationship formation that do not conform to market logic and may be distorted by attempts to apply economic analysis.

Furthermore, the framework's emphasis on competitive market dynamics may not adequately account for institutional discrimination, structural barriers, and power relationships that persist despite competitive pressures. Critics argue that labour markets, housing markets, and educational institutions are characterized by monopolistic elements, information asymmetries, and institutional barriers that prevent the competitive erosion of discrimination predicted by Becker's model (Reskin, 1998; Tomaskovic-Devey & Skaggs, 2002; Pager & Shepherd, 2008).

Despite these limitations, Becker's economic approach provides valuable theoretical insights for integration research by highlighting the role of rational calculation, market dynamics, and human capital formation in shaping integration outcomes. The framework's strength lies in its precise theoretical predictions and methodological rigour, which enable systematic empirical testing and comparison with alternative theoretical approaches (Heckman, 1998; Weiss, 1995). When combined with cultural distance theories, Becker's framework offers a complementary perspective that illuminates different aspects of the complex integration process.

Granovetter's Threshold Models: Collective Behaviour and Social Integration

Mark Granovetter's threshold models of collective behaviour provide crucial insights into how individual integration decisions aggregate into collective outcomes and how social dynamics can produce rapid shifts between integration and segregation equilibria. His seminal 1978 article 'Threshold Models of Collective Behavior' offers a theoretical framework for understanding why integration processes often exhibit nonlinear dynamics, tipping points, and unexpected collective outcomes that cannot be predicted from individual-level characteristics alone (Granovetter, 1978).

Granovetter's threshold model assumes that individuals make binary decisions about participation in collective behaviours based on the proportion of others already participating. Each individual has a threshold, i.e., the minimum proportion of others who must be participating before that individual will also participate (Granovetter, 1978). Integration can be conceptualized as a collective behaviour where immigrants and host society members decide whether to engage in cross-cultural interaction, residential integration, intermarriage, or other forms of social mixing based partly on how many others are already doing so.

Theoretical Framework and Integration Applications

The core insight of Granovetter's threshold model is that identical distributions of individual thresholds can produce dramatically different collective outcomes depending on the ordering of thresholds and initial conditions. Small changes in individual preferences or external conditions can trigger cascade effects that rapidly shift entire communities from segregated to integrated equilibria, or vice versa.

This theoretical framework provides crucial insights for understanding integration phenomena that appear puzzling from purely individual-level perspectives. Rapid neighbourhood transitions, sudden shifts in intergroup contact patterns, and the emergence or collapse of ethnic enclaves can be understood as threshold effects rather than changes in underlying individual preferences or capabilities (Schelling, 1971, 1978; Card et al., 2008).

The model's emphasis on interdependent decision-making addresses a critical limitation in both cultural distance theories and economic approaches, which typically treat individual integration decisions as independent of others' choices. Granovetter's framework recognizes that integration decisions are fundamentally social, with individuals' choices depending on their expectations about others' behaviour and the social consequences of their actions (Granovetter, 1985).

For immigrant integration research, threshold models offer theoretical predictions about how integration processes unfold at the community level. Initial pioneers who integrate despite high social costs can trigger cascade effects that make integration easier for subsequent individuals. Conversely, small increases in integration costs or decreases in benefits can trigger reverse cascades that rapidly increase segregation levels (Valente, 1995; Rogers, 2003).

The framework provides insights into why integration policies often exhibit nonlinear effectiveness. Policies that marginally reduce integration barriers may have no observable effects if they do not push enough individuals past their participation thresholds. However, policies that cross critical threshold distributions can trigger dramatic improvements in integration outcomes through cascade effects.

Empirical Evidence and Applications

Empirical applications of threshold models to integration phenomena have demonstrated the framework's explanatory power for understanding nonlinear integration dynamics. Studies of residential integration have shown that neighbourhood racial composition exhibits tipping point behaviour consistent with threshold models, with small changes in minority composition sometimes triggering rapid racial transition (Card et al., 2008; Easterly, 2009; Bayer et al., 2007).

Research on school integration has similarly documented threshold effects where the presence of critical masses of minority students affects both minority and majority students' educational outcomes and social integration patterns (Clotfelter, 2004; Hanushek et al., 2009). These findings support Granovetter's emphasis on interdependent decision-making rather than purely individual choice processes.

Studies of intergroup contact and friendship formation have found evidence of threshold effects in social integration processes. The willingness of individuals to form cross-cultural relationships appears to depend significantly on the prevalence of such relationships in their social environments, supporting the model's predictions about socially interdependent behaviour (Moody, 2001; Quillian & Campbell, 2003).

Labour market integration research has documented threshold effects in occupational integration, where the presence of ethnic minorities in particular occupations affects both the willingness of additional minorities to enter those occupations and the receptivity of employers and coworkers (Beaman, 2012). These dynamics can produce either virtuous cycles of integration or vicious cycles of segregation.

Theoretical Extensions and Complex Dynamics

Granovetter's basic threshold model has been extended by subsequent researchers to incorporate more complex social dynamics relevant to integration processes. Multidimensional threshold models examine how individuals may have different thresholds for different types of integration behaviours, leading to partial integration equilibria where groups integrate in some domains while remaining segregated in others.

Spatial threshold models incorporate geographic constraints and local interaction effects, recognizing that integration decisions often depend on the behaviour of geographically proximate individuals rather than society-wide participation rates. These models help explain the persistence of spatially clustered integration patterns and the role of residential segregation in maintaining other forms of social separation.

Dynamic threshold models examine how thresholds themselves may change over time in response to integration experiences, policy interventions, or generational replacement. These extensions address a key limitation of the basic model by allowing for endogenous preference change and learning effects that are crucial for understanding long-term integration processes.

Network-based threshold models incorporate insights from social network theory to examine how integration decisions depend on the behaviour of specific social contacts rather than aggregate participation rates. These models help explain why integration patterns often follow existing social network structures and why network-based interventions may be particularly effective for promoting integration.

Critical Limitations and Theoretical Challenges

Despite its theoretical insights, Granovetter's threshold model faces several limitations that affect its application to integration research. The model's assumption of binary choice (participate or not participate) may oversimplify integration processes that involve continuous degrees of participation across multiple domains. Real integration processes involve complex, multidimensional choice spaces that may not conform to simple threshold dynamics.

The framework's emphasis on proportion-based thresholds may not adequately capture integration dynamics that depend on absolute numbers, social network structures, or qualitative characteristics of other participants. An immigrant's integration decision may depend more on the presence of specific types of individuals (educated professionals, co-religionists, family members) than on overall participation rates.

The model's assumption of exogenous, stable thresholds conflicts with substantial evidence that integration preferences and thresholds change systematically through contact experiences, generational replacement, and policy interventions. The endogenous threshold change that characterizes real integration processes may undermine the model's predictive capacity.

Furthermore, the framework's focus on social conformity and bandwagon effects may underestimate the role of principled commitment, cultural values, and individual agency in integration decisions. Some integration behaviours may be driven by moral commitments, cultural obligations, or individual preferences that are relatively insensitive to others' participation rates.

The model's lack of attention to power relationships, institutional constraints, and structural barriers may limit its applicability to integration contexts where individual choices are constrained by discrimination, legal restrictions, or resource limitations. Threshold dynamics may operate differently when participation is involuntary or when the costs and benefits of participation are unequally distributed across groups.

Despite these limitations, Granovetter's threshold models provide valuable theoretical insights for understanding the collective dynamics of integration processes. The framework's emphasis on interdependent decision-making, nonlinear dynamics, and tipping point phenomena addresses crucial gaps in individual-level integration theories and offers insights into why integration policies often exhibit threshold effects and why integration processes can exhibit rapid, seemingly unpredictable changes (Watts, 2002; Centola, 2018). When integrated with cultural distance theories and economic approaches, threshold models contribute to a more comprehensive understanding of integration as a complex social process involving individual choices, collective dynamics, and structural constraints.

Understanding Cultural Distance in Integration Theory

This chapter discusses the nuanced terrain of cultural distance, reframing it as a vital informal institution that influences how immigrants engage with host societies. Rather than viewing integration challenges through a narrow lens of structural disadvantage, such as lack of education or limited access to employment, the text argues for the significance of cultural frameworks in shaping behaviour, social cohesion, and long-term belonging.

The chapter suggests that cultural values function as unwritten norms that shape and guide everyday social behaviour, acting as informal rules which influence how people interact and relate to one another. These unwritten codes persist in shaping outcomes, often presenting barriers that remain even when formal disadvantages are addressed. What becomes clear is that integration friction arises not merely from access to resources but from misalignments in underlying cultural expectations.

Figure 3.1 plays a critical role in visualizing this conceptual shift. It elegantly maps the spectrum of cultural distance theories, offering a comparative view of Huntington's deep civilizational divides, Hofstede's quantifiable dimensions of values, and the dynamic nature of the Inglehart-Welzel cultural clusters. It serves as a bridge between abstract theory and applied understanding, demonstrating how different frameworks interpret the same phenomenon with varying degrees of rigidity and fluidity.

Before the introduction of the figure, the discussion orients the reader towards the idea that integration must be studied beyond surface-level indicators. Cultural differences require theoretical tools that account for historic and affective attachments. Once the figure has been presented, the narrative evolves, weaving in Becker's market-based adaptations and Granovetter's network theories to stress that cultural distance is neither fixed nor absolute but shaped by incentive structures, collective memory, and evolving social patterns.

Within this framework, Huntington's theory offers a broad-brush perspective on civilization-based identity, useful in examining deep-rooted dissonance across religious and worldview lines. In contrast, Hofstede

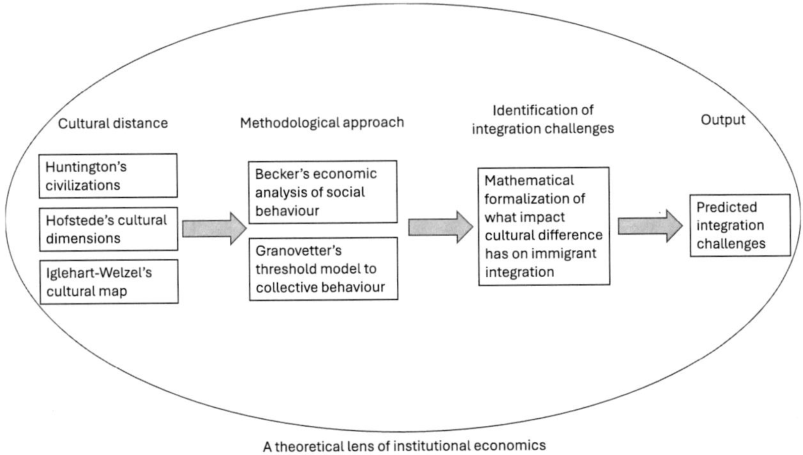

Fig. 3.1 Visualizing the theoretical landscape of immigrant integration. Source: Own elaboration

enables a more granular analysis of workplace and educational integration, measuring individualism, uncertainty avoidance, and other cultural traits. Meanwhile, the Inglehart-Welzel map highlights cultural evolution over time, revealing how values transform with increasing modernization and generational shifts.

Ultimately, the chapter makes a compelling case for the application of multiple theoretical lenses. It shows that cultural distance is not monolithic but multifaceted, and that addressing integration requires more than policy interventions; it calls for an understanding of the informal emotional and cognitive landscapes that shape how people relate across difference. These insights allow researchers and policymakers to approach integration with greater precision and empathy, moving beyond simplistic binaries and towards a more robust comprehension of cultural interplay.

References

Ager, A., & Strang, A. (2008). Understanding integration: A conceptual framework. *Journal of Refugee Studies, 21*(2), 166–191. https://doi.org/10.1093/jrs/fen016

Aigner, D. J., & Cain, G. G. (1977). Statistical theories of discrimination in labor markets. *Industrial and Labor Relations Review, 30*(2), 175–187. https://doi.org/10.2307/2522871

Ailon, G. (2008). Mirror, mirror on the wall: Culture's consequences in a value test of its own design. *Academy of Management Review, 33*(4), 885–904. https://doi.org/10.5465/amr.2008.34421995

Akerlof, G. A., & Kranton, R. E. (2000). Economics and identity. *The Quarterly Journal of Economics, 115*(3), 715–753. https://doi.org/10.1162/003355300554881

Alba, R., & Nee, V. (2003). *Remaking the American mainstream: Assimilation and contemporary immigration*. Harvard University Press.

Alesina, A., Giuliano, P., & Nunn, N. (2013). On the origins of gender roles: Women and the plough. *Quarterly Journal of Economics, 128*(2), 469–530. https://doi.org/10.1093/qje/qjt005

Appadurai, A. (1996). *Modernity at large: Cultural dimensions of globalization*. University of Minnesota Press.

Arrow, K. J. (1973). The theory of discrimination. In O. Ashenfelter & A. Rees (Eds.), *Discrimination in labor markets* (pp. 3–33). Princeton University Press.

Basic, G., & Yakhlef, S. (2025). From stigma to inclusion: Ethnographic studies in social pedagogy. *Ethnography, 16*, 1–21. https://doi.org/10.1177/14661381251352672

Bayer, P., Ferreira, F., & McMillan, R. (2007). A unified framework for measuring preferences for schools and neighborhoods. *Journal of Political Economy, 115*(4), 588–638. https://doi.org/10.1086/522381

Beaman, L. A. (2012). Social networks and the dynamics of labour market outcomes: Evidence from refugees resettled in the US. *The Review of Economic Studies, 79*(1), 128–161.

Becker, G. S. (1957). *The economics of discrimination*. University of Chicago Press.

Becker, G. S. (1964). *Human capital: A theoretical and empirical analysis, with special reference to education*. University of Chicago Press.

Becker, G. S. (1976). *The economic approach to human behavior*. University of Chicago Press.

Becker, G. S. (1991). *A treatise on the family* (Enlarged ed.). Harvard University Press.

Becker, G. S. (1993). *Human capital: A theoretical and empirical analysis, with special reference to education* (3rd ed.). University of Chicago Press.

Bhabha, H. K. (1994). *The location of culture*. Routledge.

Bisin, A., & Verdier, T. (2001). The economics of cultural transmission and the dynamics of preferences. *Journal of Economic Theory, 97*(2), 298–319. https://doi.org/10.1006/jeth.2000.2678

Blau, F. D., Kahn, L. M., Liu, A. Y. H., & Papps, K. L. (2013). The transmission of women's fertility, human capital, and work orientation across immigrant generations. *Journal of Population Economics, 26*(2), 405–435. https://doi.org/10.1007/s00148-012-0424-x

Borjas, G. J. (1999). *Heaven's door. Immigration policy and the American economy.* Princeton University Press.
Card, D. (2005). Is the new immigration really so bad? *The Economic Journal, 115*(507), F300–F323. https://doi.org/10.1111/j.1468-0297.2005.01037.x
Card, D., Mas, A., & Rothstein, J. (2008). Tipping and the dynamics of segregation. *The Quarterly Journal of Economics, 123*(1), 177–218. https://doi.org/10.1162/qjec.2008.123.1.177
Centola, D. (2018). *How behavior spreads: The science of complex contagions.* Princeton University Press.
Charles, K. K., & Guryan, J. (2008). Prejudice and wages: An empirical assessment of Becker's the economics of discrimination. *Journal of Political Economy, 116*(5), 773–809. https://doi.org/10.1086/593073
Chiswick, B. R. (1978). The effect of Americanization on the earnings of foreign-born men. *Journal of Political Economy, 86*(5), 897–921. https://doi.org/10.1086/260717
Chiswick, B. R., & Miller, P. W. (2002). Immigrant earnings: Language skills, linguistic concentrations and the business cycle. *Journal of Population Economics, 15*(1), 31–57. https://doi.org/10.1007/PL00003838
Clotfelter, C. T. (2004). *After Brown: The rise and retreat of school desegregation.* Princeton University Press.
Coleman, J. S. (1990). *Foundations of social theory.* Harvard University Press.
Creary, S. J., Caza, B. B., & Roberts, L. M. (2015). Out of the box? How managing a subordinate's multiple identities affects the quality of a manager-subordinate relationship. *Academy of Management Review, 40*(4), 538–562. https://doi.org/10.5465/amr.2013.0101
Darity, W. A., Jr., & Mason, P. L. (1998). Evidence on discrimination in employment: Codes of color, codes of gender. *Journal of Economic Perspectives, 12*(2), 63–90. https://doi.org/10.1257/jep.12.2.63
Dustmann, C., & Preston, I. P. (2007). Racial and economic factors in attitudes to immigration. *The B.E. Journal of. Economic Analysis & Policy, 7*(1), 1–39. https://doi.org/10.2202/1935-1682.1655
Easterly, W. (2009). Empirics of strategic interdependence: The case of the racial tipping point. *The B.E. Journal of Macroeconomics, 9*(1), 1–25. https://doi.org/10.2202/1935-1690.1492
Ede, L., & Starrin, B. (2014). Unresolved conflicts and shaming processes: Risk factors for long-term sick leave for mental-health reasons. *Nordic Journal of Social Research, 5*(1), 39–54. https://doi.org/10.7577/njsr.2074
Fernández, R., & Fogli, A. (2006). Fertility: The role of culture and family experience. *Journal of the European Economic Association, 4*(2–3), 552–561. https://doi.org/10.1162/jeea.2006.4.2-3.552
Galtung, J. (1969). Violence, peace, and peace research. *Journal of Peace Research, 6*(3), 167–191. https://doi.org/10.1177/002234336900600301

Gavrilets, S. (2021). Coevolution of actions, personal norms and beliefs. *Evolutionary Human Sciences, 3*, e44. https://doi.org/10.1017/ehs.2021.40
Gelfand, M. J., Gavrilets, S., & Nunn, N. (2024). Norm dynamics: Interdisciplinary perspectives on social norm emergence, persistence, and change. *Annual Review of Psychology, 75*, 341–378. https://doi.org/10.1146/annurev-psych-033020-013319
Goldin, C. (2021). *Career and family: Women's century-long journey toward equity*. Princeton University Press.
Granovetter, M. (1978). Threshold models of collective behavior. *American Journal of Sociology, 83*(6), 1420–1443. https://doi.org/10.1086/226707
Granovetter, M. (1985). Economic action and social structure: The problem of embeddedness. *American Journal of Sociology*, 91(3), 481–510. https://www.jstor.org/stable/2780199
Gudykunst, W. B., & Ting-Toomey, S. (1988). *Culture and interpersonal communication*. Sage Publications.
Guiso, L., Sapienza, P., & Zingales, L. (2006). Does culture affect economic outcomes? *Journal of Economic Perspectives, 20*(2), 23–48. https://doi.org/10.1257/jep.20.2.23
Hall, E. T. (1976). *Beyond culture*. Anchor Books.
Hall, E. T. (1983). *The dance of life: The other dimension of time*. Anchor Books.
Hanushek, E. A., Kain, J. F., & Rivkin, S. G. (2009). New evidence about Brown v. Board of Education: The complex effects of school racial composition on achievement. *Journal of Labor Economics, 27*(3), 349–383. https://doi.org/10.1086/600386
Heckman, J. J. (1998). Detecting discrimination. *Journal of Economic Perspectives, 12*(2), 101–116. https://doi.org/10.1257/jep.12.2.101
Hofstede, G. (2001). *Culture's consequences: Comparing values, Behaviors, institutions and organizations across nations*. Sage.
Hofstede, G., Hofstede, G. J., & Minkov, M. (2010). *Cultures and organizations: Software of the mind*. McGraw-Hill.
House, R. J., Hanges, P. J., Javidan, M., Dorfman, P. W., & Gupta, V. (Eds.). (2004). *Culture, leadership, and organizations: The GLOBE study of 62 societies*. Sage Publications.
Huntington, S. P. (1996). *The clash of civilizations and the remaking of world order*. Simon & Schuster.
Inglehart, R., & Norris, P. (2003). *Rising tide: Gender equality and cultural change around the world*. Cambridge University Press.
Inglehart, R. F., & Welzel, C. (2005). *Modernization, cultural change, and democracy*. Cambridge University Press.
Jones, G. (2022). *The culture transplant. How migrants make the economies they move to a lot like the ones they left*. Stanford University Press.

Kelman, H. C. (2008). A social-psychological approach to conflict analysis and resolution. In D. Sandole, S. Byrne, I. Sandole-Staroste, & J. Seheni (Eds.), *Handbook of conflict analysis and resolution* (pp. 170–183). Routledge.

Kingston, C., & Caballero, G. (2009). Comparing theories of institutional change. *Journal of Institutional Economics, 5*(2), 151–180. https://doi.org/10.1017/S1744137409001283

Lackey, D. P. (1989). *The ethics of war and peace*. Prentice Hall.

Lamont, M., & Molnar, V. (2002). The study of boundaries in the social sciences. *Annual Review of Sociology, 28*(1), 167–195. https://doi.org/10.1146/annurev.soc.28.110601.141107

Lang, K., & Lehmann, J. Y. K. (2012). Racial discrimination in the labor market: Theory and empirics. *Journal of Economic Literature, 50*(4), 959–1006. https://doi.org/10.1257/jel.50.4.959

Lazić, M., & Pešić, J. (2024). Values, norms and social dynamics. *Philosophy and Society, 35*(3), 703–724. https://doi.org/10.2298/FID2403703L

Levine, R. (1997). *A geography of time: The temporal misadventures of a social psychologist*. Basic Books.

March, J. G., & Olsen, J. P. (1986). Popular sovereignty and the search for appropriate institutions. *Journal of Public Policy, 6*(4), 341–370. https://doi.org/10.1017/S0143814X00004207

March, J. G., & Olsen, J. P. (1989). *Rediscovering institutions. The organizational basis of politics*. Free Press.

Markus, H. R., & Kitayama, S. (1991). Culture and the self: Implications for cognition, emotion, and motivation. *Psychological Review, 98*(2), 224–253. https://doi.org/10.1037/0033-295X.98.2.224

McSweeney, B. (2002). Hofstede's model of national cultural differences and their consequences: A triumph of faith - a failure of analysis. *Human Relations, 55*, 89–118. https://doi.org/10.1177/0018726702551004

Michalak, L., & Trocki, K. (2006). Alcohol and Islam: An overview. *Contemporary Drug Problems, 33*(4), 523–562. https://doi.org/10.1177/009145090603300401

Milgrom, P., North, D., & Weingast, B. (1990). The role of institutions in the revival of trade: The law merchant, private judges and the champagne fairs. *Economics and Politics, 2*(1), 1–23. https://doi.org/10.1111/j.1468-0343.1990.tb00020.x

Moody, J. (2001). Race, school integration, and friendship segregation in America. *American Journal of Sociology, 107*(3), 679–716. https://doi.org/10.1086/338954

North, D. C. (1990). *Institutions, institutional change and economic performance*. Cambridge University Press.

North, D. C. (1991). Institutions. *Journal of Economic Perspectives, 5*(1), 97–112. https://doi.org/10.1257/jep.5.1.97

North, D. C., & Thomas, R. P. (1973). *The rise of the Western world. A new economic history*. Cambridge University Press.

OECD. (2024). *The economic case for greater LGBTI+ equality in the United States*. OECD Publishing. https://doi.org/10.1787/5adfe3a5-en

Pager, D., & Shepherd, H. (2008). The sociology of discrimination: Racial discrimination in employment, housing, credit, and consumer markets. *Annual Review of Sociology, 34*, 181–209. https://doi.org/10.1146/annurev.soc.33.040406.131740

Penninx, R. (2003). *Integration: The role of communities, institutions and the state*. Migration Policy Institute, October 1, 2003. Retrieved August 17, 2025, from www.migrationpolicy.org

Phelps, E. S. (1972). The statistical theory of racism and sexism. *The American Economic Review, 62*(4), 659–661.

Portes, A., & Rumbaut, R. G. (2001). *Legacies: The story of the immigrant second generation*. University of California Press.

Quillian, L., & Campbell, M. E. (2003). Beyond black and white: The present and future of multiracial friendship segregation. *American Sociological Review, 68*(4), 540–566. https://doi.org/10.2307/1519738

Rauhut, D. (2020). *Integration and informal institutions*. *Society, 57*(2), 211–218. https://doi.org/10.1007/s12115-020-00467-6

Rauhut, D. (2026a). Rethinking immigrant integration theories for the 21st century. In B. Newbold & M. Crea-Arsenio (Eds.), *A research agenda for immigration settlement and adjustment* (pp. 9–29). Edward Elgar.

Rauhut, D. (2026b). A dynamic model of immigrant integration: Structure, agency and mutual willingness. *International Migration, 64*(2), e70154. https://doi.org/10.1111/imig.70154

Rauhut, D., & Laine, J. P. (2023). Crossing the border: Immigrant integration in a bordering perspective. In D. Rauhut (Ed.), *New methods and theory on immigrant integration: Insights from remote and peripheral areas* (pp. 68–85). Edward Elgar.

Reskin, B. (1998). *The realities of affirmative action in employment*. American Sociological Association.

Rogers, E. M. (2003). *Diffusion of innovations* (5th ed.). Free Press.

Room, R., & Mäkelä, K. (2000). Typologies of the cultural position of drinking. *Journal of Studies on Alcohol, 61*(3), 475–483. https://doi.org/10.15288/jsa.2000.61.475

Rosenberg, N., & Birdzell, L. E., Jr. (1986). *How the west grew rich: The economic transformation of the industrial world*. Basic Books.

Rothstein, B., & Stolle, D. (2008). The state and social capital: An institutional theory of generalized trust. *Comparative Politics, 40*(4), 441–459. https://doi.org/10.5129/001041508X12911362383354

Said, E. W. (2001). The clash of ignorance. *The Nation, 273*(12), 11–13.

Schelling, T. C. (1971). Dynamic models of segregation. *Journal of Mathematical Sociology, 1*(2), 143–186. https://doi.org/10.1080/0022250X.1971.9989794
Schelling, T. C. (1978). *Micromotives and macrobehavior.* W.W. Norton & Company.
Schwartz, S. J., Unger, J. B., Zamboanga, B. L., & Szapocznik, J. (2010). Rethinking the concept of acculturation: Implications for theory and research. *American Psychologist, 65*(4), 237–251. https://doi.org/10.1037/a0019330
Searle, J. R. (2005). What is an institution? *Journal of Institutional Economics, 1*(1), 1–22. https://doi.org/10.1017/S1744137405000020
Sen, A. (2006). *Identity and violence: The illusion of destiny.* W.W. Norton & Company.
Shore, L. M., Cleveland, J. N., & Sanchez, D. (2018). Inclusive workplaces: A review and model. *Human Resource Management Review, 28*(2), 176–189. https://doi.org/10.1016/j.hrmr.2017.07.003
Stark, O. (1991). *The migration of labor.* Blackwell.
Ting-Toomey, S. (1988). Intercultural conflict styles: A face-negotiation theory. In Y. Y. Kim & W. B. Gudykunst (Eds.), *Theories in intercultural communication* (pp. 213–235). Sage Publications.
Tomaskovic-Devey, D., & Skaggs, S. (2002). Sex segregation, labor process organization, and gender earnings inequality. *American Journal of Sociology, 108*(1), 102–128. https://doi.org/10.1086/344214
Transparency International. (2020). *Corruption perceptions index 2020.* Transparency International.
Triandis, H. C. (2018). *Individualism and collectivism.* Westview Press.
Uslaner, E. M. (2002). *The moral foundations of trust.* Cambridge University Press.
Valente, T. W. (1995). Network models of the diffusion of innovations. *Computational and Mathematical Organization Theory, 2*(2), 163–164. https://doi.org/10.1007/BF00240425
Watts, D. J. (2002). A simple model of global cascades on random networks. *Proceedings of the National Academy of Sciences, 99*(9), 5766–5771. https://doi.org/10.1073/pnas.082090499
Weiss, A. (1995). Human capital vs. signalling explanations of wages. *Journal of Economic Perspectives, 9*(4), 133–154. https://doi.org/10.1257/jep.9.4.133
Williamson, O. E. (2000). The new institutional economics: Taking stock, looking ahead. *Journal of Economic Literature, 38*(3), 595–613. https://doi.org/10.1257/jel.38.3.595
World Bank. (2012). *World development report 2012: Gender equality and development.* Retrieved October 3, 2025, from https://openknowledge.worldbank.org/entities/publication/51c285f6-0200-590c-97d3-95b937be3271
Zhou, M., & Bankston, C. L. (1998). *Growing up American: How Vietnamese children adapt to life in the United States.* Russell Sage Foundation.

CHAPTER 4

Towards an Integrated Framework

The analysis of Huntington's civilizational theory, Hofstede's cultural dimensions, and the Inglehart-Welzel cultural map reveals complementary insights into how cultural differences affect integration processes. While each framework captures important aspects of cultural variation, none alone provides a complete theoretical foundation for understanding the relationship between cultural distance and integration outcomes. This section develops an integrated *Cultural Distance Integration Model* (CDIM) that synthesizes insights from all three approaches while addressing their individual limitations.

The CDIM proposes that cultural distance operates as a multidimensional construct affecting integration through three primary mechanisms: *cognitive dissonance, social coordination difficulties*, and *institutional incompatibilities.* These mechanisms interact across different levels of cultural difference (civilizational, dimensional, and developmental) to create varying degrees of integration challenge. Crucially, the model theorizes the existence of *cultural distance thresholds* beyond which successful integration becomes systematically improbable within reasonable timeframes.

D. Rauhut, *Institutional Economics and Immigrant Integration*, https://doi.org/10.1007/978-3-032-28361-0_4

The Three-Level Architecture of Cultural Distance

The first level addresses civilizational foundations (Deep Structure). Drawing from Huntington's framework, the deepest level of cultural distance involves fundamental differences in civilizational worldviews. These differences affect basic cognitive categories, ultimate values, and core assumptions about human nature, social organization, and the proper relationship between individual and collective, sacred and secular, tradition and change (Berger & Luckmann, 1966). Civilizational differences create a *worldview incompatibility*, i.e., a systematic difference in how social reality is perceived, categorized, and evaluated. The theoretical model proposes that civilizational distance affects integration through deep cognitive mechanisms. When immigrants and host populations operate from different civilizational foundations, they literally inhabit different symbolic universes with incompatible meaning systems (Schutz, 1967). This creates fundamental communication barriers that extend beyond language to encompass basic assumptions about causation, morality, authority, and social relationships. Civilizational incompatibility manifests in several theoretical patterns:

- Interpretive dissonance: The same behaviours, institutions, or social arrangements are interpreted through incompatible meaning frameworks, leading to systematic misunderstanding and conflict.
- Value incommensurability: Core values from different civilizational traditions cannot be easily ranked, compared, or integrated because they rest on different foundational assumptions about human flourishing and social good (MacIntyre, 1988).
- Identity conflict: Individuals experience psychological tension when civilizational identity conflicts with practical requirements for host society participation, leading to what Huntington terms 'cultural schizophrenia'.

The second level addresses dimensional variations (Behavioural Patterns). Hofstede's cultural dimensions operate at an intermediate level, capturing variations in behavioural patterns, social practices, and organizational preferences within broadly compatible civilizational frameworks. These differences affect *social coordination mechanisms*, i.e., the ability of individuals from different cultural backgrounds to interact effectively, form relationships, and participate in common institutions.

The theoretical model proposes that dimensional distance creates *coordination failures* across multiple domains. Large gaps in power distance affect authority relationships in educational, workplace, and civic contexts. Individualism-collectivism differences create incompatible expectations about social obligations, decision-making processes, and relationship formation. Uncertainty avoidance variations affect adaptation to institutional flexibility and tolerance for cultural diversity.

Dimensional incompatibility operates through several mechanisms:

- Behavioural misalignment: Different cultural programming leads to behavioural patterns that are systematically inappropriate or ineffective in the host society context (Triandis, 1995).
- Expectation conflicts: Incompatible expectations about appropriate behaviour in social roles create frustration, misunderstanding, and relationship breakdown.
- Institutional friction: Cultural dimensions that conflict with host society institutional assumptions create systematic difficulties in educational, workplace, and civic participation.

The third level addresses the developmental position (Societal Values). The Inglehart-Welzel framework captures a third level of cultural distance related to a society's position in the broader modernization and human development process. These differences affect *institutional compatibility*, i.e., the degree to which immigrant cultural orientations align with host society institutional frameworks, political systems, and social norms.

Developmental distance creates *institutional incompatibilities* when immigrant populations carry value orientations that conflict with the fundamental assumptions underlying host society institutions. Traditional-oriented immigrants in secular-rational societies face conflicts over the role of religion in public life, family authority structures, and individual autonomy. Survival-oriented immigrants in self-expression societies encounter difficulties with democratic participation, lifestyle tolerance, and work-life balance expectations.

The theoretical model identifies several institutional incompatibility patterns:

- Legal system conflicts: Traditional values regarding family authority, gender roles, or religious obligations conflict with host society legal frameworks emphasizing individual rights and gender equality.

- Democratic participation barriers: Survival-oriented political cultures conflict with self-expression democratic norms requiring tolerance, debate, and individual political expression.
- Social integration difficulties: Traditional survival orientations conflict with host society emphasis on individual choice, lifestyle diversity, and subjective wellbeing.

The Cultural Distance Threshold Hypothesis

The central theoretical innovation of the CDIM is the *Cultural Distance Threshold Hypothesis*, which proposes that cultural distance effects on integration are not linear but exhibit threshold properties. Below certain thresholds, cultural differences create manageable adaptation challenges that can be overcome through normal integration processes. Beyond these thresholds, cultural distance creates systematic barriers that cannot be easily bridged within reasonable timeframes using standard integration approaches.

The threshold concept draws on cognitive psychology research demonstrating that human information processing capabilities have finite limits (Miller, 1956; Kahneman, 1973). When cultural differences require simultaneous adaptation across multiple domains and levels, they may exceed the cognitive and social adaptive capacity of both immigrants and host society institutions.

The model proposes three types of thresholds: (1) *Individual cognitive thresholds*: beyond certain levels of cultural distance, individuals cannot simultaneously maintain psychological coherence while adapting to fundamentally incompatible cultural requirements. This creates what Festinger (1957) termed 'cognitive dissonance' at levels that become psychologically unsustainable. (2) *Social interaction thresholds*: when cultural differences affect multiple dimensions of social interaction simultaneously, they create coordination problems that cannot be resolved through normal social learning processes. Interactions become systematically difficult rather than merely requiring adjustment periods. (3) *Institutional absorption thresholds:* host society institutions have finite capacity to accommodate cultural diversity without losing their essential characteristics or functional effectiveness. Beyond certain levels of cultural distance, institutional adaptation requirements become so extensive that they threaten institutional integrity.

The CDIM proposes that thresholds operate not just within single levels but through *cross-level interaction effects*. When cultural distance is high across multiple levels simultaneously (civilizational, dimensional, and developmental), the threshold effects are multiplicative rather than additive. This explains why some cultural distances appear particularly problematic for integration while others of similar magnitude create fewer difficulties.

For example, immigration from societies that differ across all three levels (different civilization, opposite cultural dimensions, and distant developmental position) creates what the model terms *compound cultural distance*. Such compound distance may exceed multiple thresholds simultaneously, creating integration challenges that are qualitatively different from and more severe than the sum of individual-level effects.

Mechanisms of Cultural Distance Effects

Cultural distance affects integration through cognitive mechanisms that operate at both conscious and unconscious levels. When immigrants encounter host society cultural requirements that conflict with deep-seated cultural programming, they experience cognitive dissonance that can manifest in several patterns:

1. Identity fragmentation: Individuals may develop compartmentalized identities, maintaining traditional cultural orientations in private spheres while adopting host society behaviours in public contexts. While this may appear to facilitate integration, it often creates psychological stress and prevents the deep cultural learning necessary for genuine integration (LaFromboise et al., 1993).
2. Selective adaptation: Immigrants may adapt selectively to host society requirements while maintaining strong resistance to changes in core cultural domains. This pattern can create persistent integration difficulties in areas where cultural change is necessary for effective participation.
3. Cultural rejection: When cultural distance creates excessive cognitive dissonance, individuals may reject host society cultural requirements entirely, leading to voluntary segregation and oppositional identity formation (Ogbu, 1991).

Cultural distance affects the fundamental social processes through which relationships are formed, maintained, and utilized for social and economic advancement. Large cultural distances create several coordination problems:

1. Communication breakdown: Beyond simple language barriers, cultural distance creates systematic miscommunication where the same words, gestures, or behaviours carry different meanings and implications across cultural groups (Hall, 1976). This affects relationship formation, workplace interactions, and civic participation.
2. Trust deficits: Social trust depends partly on predictability and shared understanding of behavioural norms (Coleman, 1990). Large cultural distances reduce predictability and create suspicion about motivations and intentions, impeding the social relationship formation necessary for integration.
3. Network segregation: When cross-cultural social coordination becomes consistently difficult, both immigrants and host society members may retreat into culturally homogeneous social networks, reducing opportunities for integration and cultural learning (McPherson et al., 2001).

The most visible and politically consequential effects of cultural distance operate through conflicts between immigrant cultural requirements and host society institutional frameworks. These conflicts occur across multiple institutional domains:

1. Educational system conflicts: Large cultural distances create systematic conflicts between immigrant family cultural requirements and educational system assumptions about appropriate pedagogy, parent-child relationships, gender roles, and individual autonomy. These conflicts affect not only individual educational outcomes but institutional capacity to serve culturally diverse populations effectively.
2. Legal system incompatibilities: When immigrant cultural practices conflict with host society legal frameworks, particularly in areas of family law, gender relations, and religious expression, the result is often zero-sum conflicts where accommodation of cultural difference requires fundamental changes to legal principles or immigrant cultural practices (Shachar, 2001).

3. Workplace integration barriers: Cultural dimensions that affect authority relationships, communication styles, and work-life balance create systematic workplace integration difficulties that cannot be resolved through standard diversity training or accommodation approaches.

The Bidirectional Nature of Cultural Distance Effects

A crucial insight of the CDIM is that cultural distance effects are *bidirectional*, i.e., they affect both immigrant adaptation and host society responses. Previous integration theories have often focused primarily on immigrant adaptation while treating host society characteristics as fixed parameters. However, immigration and the culture, norms, and values they carry have an impact on the host society (Jones, 2022). The CDIM recognizes that integration success depends on adaptive processes occurring in both directions. Yet adaptation does not occur solely within policy or institutional frameworks; it also plays out through symbolic interaction and the negotiation of boundary positions.

These mutual adaptation processes unfold not only through policy mechanisms or institutional design but also through the micropolitics of interaction, i.e., how immigrants and host populations cross, maintain, or resist socially constructed boundaries. As Rauhut and Laine (2023) argue, integration is inseparable from bordering, a dynamic process in which symbolic, psychological, and institutional lines demarcate who belongs and under what conditions. These borders are not static but co-produced through spatial arrangements, discursive framings, and interpersonal negotiations. In this sense, the bidirectional nature of integration is not just behavioural or institutional; it is boundary-political. Mutual adaptation requires not only accommodation of cultural differences but also active dismantling of exclusionary frames that inhibit the formation of bridging ties (Rauhut, 2026).

Large cultural distances require host society institutions to make significant adaptations to accommodate cultural diversity effectively. These adaptation requirements have theoretical limits that vary across institutional domains and cultural characteristics of host societies. (1) Institutional flexibility limits: different institutions have varying capacities for cultural accommodation without losing essential characteristics. Educational systems may have greater flexibility than legal systems, which must maintain consistency and predictability to function effectively. (2) Cultural tolerance thresholds: host society populations have varying tolerance for cultural difference, with tolerance potentially decreasing as cultural distance increases and accommodation requirements become more extensive (Blalock, 1967). (3) Democratic legitimacy constraints: in democratic societies, extensive institutional adaptations to accommodate cultural minorities require majority support or at least acquiescence. Large cultural distances may generate majority resistance that creates political barriers to necessary institutional adaptations.

Successful integration of culturally distant populations requires *mutual adaptation processes* where both immigrants and host societies undergo cultural change. The CDIM proposes that these processes have optimal ranges; too little mutual adaptation fails to bridge cultural distances, while too much threatens the cultural integrity of both groups. The model identifies several mutual adaptation patterns: (1) convergent adaptation: both groups move towards intermediate cultural positions that preserve essential cultural elements while enabling effective interaction and institutional participation. (2) Parallel adaptation: groups maintain distinct cultural characteristics while developing shared frameworks for interaction in public spheres. (3) Sequential adaptation: different aspects of cultural difference are addressed through adaptation processes occurring over extended timeframes, allowing gradual cultural change that avoids excessive disruption.

Temporal Dynamics and Generational Effects

The CDIM incorporates temporal dimensions that are often neglected in integration theory. Cultural distance effects operate differently across timeframes, with some effects immediate and others emerging only over generational periods. Drawing on insights from the Inglehart-Welzel framework, the model proposes that successful integration of culturally distant populations often requires *generational cultural change processes*. First-generation immigrants may maintain strong cultural orientations from origin societies while adapting behaviourally to host society requirements. Successful integration may depend on second and subsequent generations developing cultural orientations more compatible with host society institutional requirements.

This temporal dimension has important implications for evaluating integration success. Cultural distance effects that appear insurmountable within single generations may be resolved through intergenerational processes, but only if conditions support gradual cultural change rather than cultural entrenchment or oppositional identity formation.

The model incorporates insights from cultural transmission theory (Cavalli-Sforza & Feldman, 1981) to understand how cultural distance affects intergenerational cultural change. Large cultural distances may actually impede intergenerational cultural adaptation by creating conditions that encourage cultural preservation rather than cultural change.

When parents perceive host society cultural requirements as threatening to essential cultural values, they may intensify cultural transmission efforts to preserve traditional orientations in subsequent generations. This can create *cultural entrenchment* patterns where cultural distance persists or even increases across generations rather than decreasing through natural adaptation processes.

Spatial Dynamics and the Amplification of Cultural Distance

The influence of cultural distance on immigrant integration is not merely a matter of individual characteristics or abstract value divergence; it unfolds within spatially bounded social environments that shape the degree and manner in which cultural distance manifests. Spatial distribution patterns of immigrants with culturally divergent norms, values, and preferences and how they are geographically located within host societies play a pivotal role in modulating the mechanisms of integration outlined in preceding sections. While cultural distance operates at the civilizational, dimensional, and developmental levels, its effects are intensified or attenuated by spatial arrangements that govern intergroup contact, institutional access, and social learning opportunities.

Residential clustering among culturally distant immigrant groups can produce what Vertovec (2007) has termed 'superdiverse' urban formations. However, these formations do not necessarily foster intercultural exchange. Rather, when cultural enclaves develop in socioeconomically deprived or spatially segregated areas, they may result in parallel societies characterized by limited interaction with the host majority (Musterd, 2005). Such spatial configurations may inhibit bridging social capital, impeding the development of mutual trust and social cohesion (Putnam, 2007). The emergence of these parallel structures magnifies coordination difficulties and institutional incompatibilities, as the enclave's cultural logics evolve in relative isolation from dominant societal norms.

Indeed, proximity alone does not guarantee integration. Mere co-location without meaningful interaction may perpetuate stereotypes, misunderstandings, and social distance. Here, the quality of contact matters as much as its frequency. Pettigrew (1998) stresses that structured, cooperative, and status-equal interactions are more likely to reduce prejudice and enable cultural accommodation. Spatial arrangements that concentrate culturally distant groups in homogeneous zones reduce the probability of such contact, particularly when physical segregation coincides with symbolic boundaries.

The temporality of spatial settlement patterns further complicates integration trajectories. Early settlement choices, often dictated by affordability and migrant networks, tend to produce high concentrations of culturally similar groups. Over time, these concentrations may entrench cultural distance by creating 'localised cultural infrastructures' that reproduce origin country norms in host society settings (Phillips et al., 2007). This has implications for generational integration, as second-generation immigrants socialized in these environments may experience delayed or selective adaptation relative to their peers in more mixed areas.

The spatialization of cultural distance thus constitutes a fourth tier of influence, complementing and interacting with the civilizational, dimensional, and developmental dimensions. Understanding cultural distance in situ requires attending to how physical geographies shape social geographies of integration.

Scope Conditions and Contextual Factors

The CDIM recognizes that cultural distance effects are moderated by various contextual factors that affect threshold levels and mechanism operations. These scope conditions help explain why similar cultural distances may have different integration outcomes across different contexts. *Economic opportunities* affect cultural distance tolerance by providing incentives for cultural adaptation and creating positive-sum interactions between culturally different groups (Borjas, 1999). Strong economic opportunity structures may raise cultural distance thresholds by providing material incentives for overcoming cultural coordination difficulties. Host society *institutional characteristics* significantly affect cultural distance thresholds. Institutions designed with cultural diversity in mind may accommodate larger cultural distances than those assuming cultural homogeneity. However, institutional flexibility has limits that vary across institutional types and cultural characteristics. *Demographic aspects* such as the size and concentration of culturally distant immigrant populations affect integration dynamics through several mechanisms. Small, dispersed populations may face different adaptation pressures than large, concentrated populations that can maintain separate institutional systems (Lazear, 1999). *Historical relationships* between origin and host societies, contemporary political relations, and broader political contexts significantly affect integration processes. Cultural distances may be more difficult to bridge when they occur within contexts of political conflict or historical antagonism.

Policy Interventions as Modulators of Cultural Distance Effects

While the Cultural Distance Integration Model (CDIM) primarily conceptualizes cultural distance as a set of multi-level structural differences between immigrant and host societies, it also recognizes that these differences do not operate in a vacuum. Rather, their effects on integration outcomes are systematically mediated by the presence and quality of public policy interventions. The integration impact of cultural distance is not wholly deterministic; it is conditional upon the state's capacity and willingness to intervene in ways that mitigate dissonance, enhance coordination, and align institutional interfaces.

In the CDIM framework, policy interventions function as *corrective mechanisms* that interact with the three primary integration challenges outlined earlier: *cognitive dissonance*, *social coordination difficulty*, and *institutional incompatibility*. Each of these mechanisms introduces barriers at specific societal levels (individual, communal, and systemic), yet all are modifiable through targeted policy action. The model thereby diverges from purely structural theories and incorporates an actionable domain of state agency within its theoretical architecture.

Crucially, CDIM posits that the effectiveness of policy interventions is not uniform across different cultural distance zones. In low-distance contexts, standard policy tools, such as language training, employment support, and civic education, often suffice to facilitate integration. However, as cultural distance approaches identified thresholds, these standard interventions exhibit *diminishing returns*. This necessitates a recalibration of policy architecture, including the development of mechanism-specific and culturally sensitive programmes.

For example, cognitive dissonance arising from civilizational divergence may be partially alleviated through intercultural mentorship schemes, narrative-based integration programmes, and mental health services tailored for acculturative stress (Berry, 2006). Coordination difficulties related to mismatched social norms are more effectively addressed through structured intercultural dialogue platforms, cooperative housing models, or community-based social capital initiatives (Cantle, 2012; Putnam, 2007). Institutional incompatibilities, particularly in the legal and educational domains, demand norm-translational mediation services, adapted pedagogical tools, and legal outreach programmes that clarify rights and responsibilities across cultural frames (Bloemraad, 2006; Shachar, 2001).

The integration of policy into CDIM further enhances its predictive capacity. By introducing parameters for policy intensity, targeting precision, and institutional flexibility, the model becomes capable of simulating *policy responsiveness to cultural variation*. This not only bridges the theoretical and applied dimensions of immigrant integration but also responds to Rauhut's (2023) call for an epistemology that supports the policy translation of theoretical insight.

Moreover, the inclusion of policy as a dynamic variable aligns CDIM with emerging literatures on *adaptive integration governance* and *multi-level migration management* (Goodman, 2014; Joppke, 2007). It allows for the possibility of *temporally sequenced*, *domain-specific*, and *demographically differentiated* policy strategies, such as gender-responsive programming (Anthias, 2012; Kofman, 2004) and generation-sensitive resource allocation (Portes & Rumbaut, 2001).

In sum, policy intervention is not merely a downstream response to integration failure. Within the CDIM architecture, it is conceptualized as a *co-evolutionary force*, i.e., one that acts not only upon immigrants but also upon host society institutions. The mutual adaptation pathway, foundational to CDIM's bidirectional logic, is inherently dependent on policy as a structuring medium. Where cultural distance erects boundaries, policy, if designed with precision, can build bridges.

Summary

This chapter introduces the Cultural Distance Integration Model (CDIM), a sophisticated framework designed to capture how cultural differences influence immigrant integration. Unlike singular approaches, CDIM integrates Huntington's civilizational theory, Hofstede's cultural dimensions, and the Inglehart-Welzel cultural map to reveal how these distinct perspectives interact across varying cultural levels.

At its foundation, the model identifies three core mechanisms that cultural distance impacts: cognitive dissonance, social coordination difficulties, and institutional incompatibilities (see Fig. 4.1). These emerge across three tiers (deep civilizational worldviews, behavioural dimensions, and developmental value orientations) which collectively shape the degree of cultural integration challenge.

The deepest level pertains to civilizational distance, where divergent symbolic universes cause interpretive dissonance, identity conflicts, and value incommensurability. This is followed by dimensional differences in behavioural norms, such as authority relations and risk tolerance, which affect everyday coordination and expectations. The third level tackles developmental disparities in values shaped by modernization processes, generating tension around legal norms, democratic participation, and lifestyle freedoms.

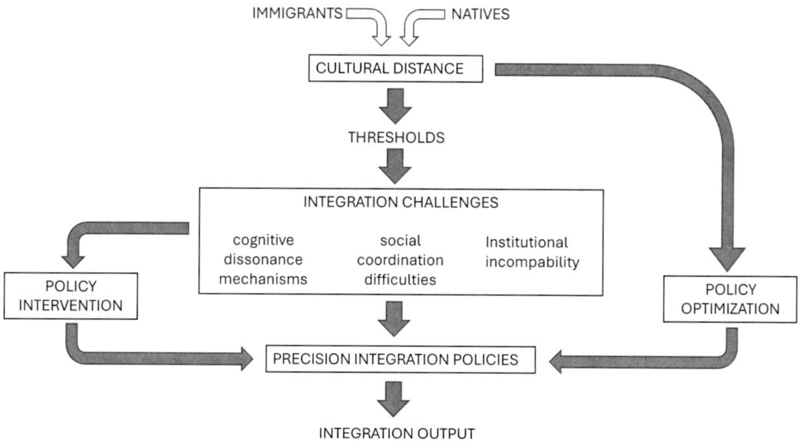

Fig. 4.1 The cultural distance framework. Source: Own elaboration

Crucially, the CDIM posits the existence of cultural distance thresholds, beyond which integration becomes significantly less feasible within conventional timescales. These thresholds operate on cognitive, social, and institutional levels, often interacting in multiplicative rather than additive ways. For example, immigrants from societies diverging on all three levels present compound cultural distance, which far exceeds what either host societies or immigrant communities can easily reconcile.

The model also accounts for the bidirectional nature of integration, arguing that successful outcomes require mutual adaptation rather than unilateral assimilation. This includes the renegotiation of cultural boundaries in public discourse and spatial arrangements. Indeed, spatial factors such as residential clustering amplify or mitigate cultural distance effects, often entrenching norms through parallel societal structures.

To manage these challenges, CDIM highlights the strategic role of policy interventions. Standard programmes may suffice when cultural distance is minimal, but high-distance contexts necessitate targeted and culturally sensitive policies, such as intercultural mentorships, norm-translational services, and adaptive pedagogies. Policies do not merely manage integration but actively shape mutual adaptation pathways.

Ultimately, the model recognizes that integration is both a temporal and a generational process. First-generation immigrants may adapt selectively, while subsequent generations engage in deeper cultural learning, i.e., provided conditions encourage cultural change rather than preservation. Gender plays a pivotal role in this dynamic, with integration experiences often stratified along gendered lines. Women, for instance, may face distinct challenges and opportunities depending on the host society's labour market structures, social norms, and policy support for childcare and family life. Simultaneously, gender expectations from origin cultures may influence both the pace and pathway of adaptation, particularly in areas such as education, employment, and civic participation. Spatial, economic, institutional, and historical contexts all modulate how cultural distance manifests, making CDIM not just a conceptual model but a diagnostic lens for understanding the evolving landscape of integration.

References

Anthias, F. (2012). Transnational mobilities, migration research and intersectionality. *Nordic Journal of Migration Research, 2*(2), 102–110. https://doi.org/10.2478/v10202-011-0032-y

Berger, P. L., & Luckmann, T. (1966). *The social construction of reality: A treatise in the sociology of knowledge*. Penguin.

Berry, J. W. (2006). Acculturation: Living successfully in two cultures. *International Journal of Intercultural Relations, 29*(6), 697–712. https://doi.org/10.1016/j.ijintrel.2005.07.013

Blalock, H. M. (1967). *Toward a theory of minority-group relations.* John Wiley & Sons.

Bloemraad, I. (2006). *Becoming a citizen: Incorporating immigrants and refugees in the United States and Canada*. University of California Press.

Borjas, G. J. (1999). *Heaven's door. Immigration policy and the American economy.* Princeton University Press.

Cantle, T. (2012). *Interculturalism: The new era of cohesion and diversity.* Palgrave Macmillan.

Cavalli-Sforza, L. L., & Feldman, M. W. (1981). *Cultural transmission and evolution: A quantitative approach.* Princeton University Press.

Coleman, J. S. (1990). *Foundations of social theory.* Harvard University Press.

Festinger, L. (1957). *A theory of cognitive dissonance.* Stanford University Press.

Goodman, S. W. (2014). *Immigration and membership politics in Western Europe.* Cambridge University Press.

Hall, E. T. (1976). *Beyond culture.* Anchor Books.

Jones, G. (2022). *The culture transplant. How migrants make the economies they move to a lot like the ones they left.* Stanford University Press.

Joppke, C. (2007). Beyond national models: Civic integration policies for immigrants in Western Europe. *West European Politics, 30*(1), 1–22. https://doi.org/10.1080/01402380601019613

Kahneman, D. (1973). *Attention and effort.* Prentice-Hall.

Kofman, E. (2004). Gendered global migrations. *International Feminist Journal of Politics, 6*(4), 643–665. https://doi.org/10.1080/1461674042000283408

LaFromboise, T., Coleman, H. L., & Gerton, J. (1993). Psychological impact of biculturalism: Evidence and theory. *Psychological Bulletin, 114*(3), 395–412. https://doi.org/10.1037/0033-2909.114.3.395

Lazear, E. P. (1999). Culture and language. *Journal of Political Economy, 107*(S6), S95–S126. https://doi.org/10.1086/250105

MacIntyre, A. (1988). *Whose justice? Which rationality?* University of Notre Dame Press.

McPherson, M., Smith-Lovin, L., & Cook, J. M. (2001). Birds of a feather: Homophily in social networks. *Annual Review of Sociology, 27*, 415–444. https://doi.org/10.1146/annurev.soc.27.1.415

Miller, G. A. (1956). The magical number seven, plus or minus two: Some limits on our capacity for processing information. *Psychological Review, 63*(2), 81–97. https://doi.org/10.1037/h0043158

Musterd, S. (2005). Social and ethnic segregation in Europe: Levels, causes, and effects. *Journal of Urban Affairs, 27*(3), 331–348. https://doi.org/10.1111/j.0735-2166.2005.00239.x

Ogbu, J. U. (1991). Immigrant and involuntary minorities in comparative perspective. In M. A. Gibson & J. U. Ogbu (Eds.), *Minority status and schooling: A comparative study of immigrant and involuntary minorities* (pp. 3–33). Garland Publishing.

Pettigrew, T. F. (1998). Intergroup contact theory. *Annual Review of Psychology, 49*(1), 65–85. https://doi.org/10.1146/annurev.psych.49.1.65

Phillips, D., Davis, C., & Ratcliffe, P. (2007). *Community cohesion and housing: A review of the evidence.* Joseph Rowntree Foundation.

Portes, A., & Rumbaut, R. G. (2001). *Legacies: The story of the immigrant second generation.* University of California Press.

Putnam, R. (2007). E pluribus unum: Diversity and community in the twenty-first century. *Scandinavian Political Studies, 30*(2), 137–174. https://doi.org/10.1111/j.1467-9477.2007.00176.x

Rauhut, D. (2023). The methodology of immigrant integration: An epistemological perspective. In D. Rauhut (Ed.), *New methods and theory on immigrant integration: Insights from remote and peripheral areas* (pp. 142–162). Edward Elgar Publishing.

Rauhut, D. (2026). A dynamic model of immigrant integration: Structure, agency and mutual willingness. *International Migration, 64*(2), e70154. https://doi.org/10.1111/imig.70154

Rauhut, D., & Laine, J. (2023). Crossing the border: Immigrant integration in a bordering perspective. In D. Rauhut (Ed.), *New methods and theory on immigrant integration: Insights from remote and peripheral areas* (pp. 68–85). Edward Elgar Publishing.

Schutz, A. (1967). *The phenomenology of the social world.* Northwestern University Press.

Shachar, A. (2001). *Multicultural jurisdictions: Cultural differences and women's rights.* Cambridge University Press.

Triandis, H. C. (1995). *Individualism and collectivism.* Routledge.

Vertovec, S. (2007). Super-diversity and its implications. *Ethnic and Racial Studies, 30*(6), 1024–1054. https://doi.org/10.1080/01419870701599465

CHAPTER 5

Mathematical Formalization of the Cultural Distance Integration Model

Introduction

The integration of immigrants into host societies represents one of the most complex and consequential social processes of our time. As global migration continues to increase, understanding the mechanisms that facilitate or hinder successful integration has become critical for policymakers, researchers, and societies worldwide. While numerous theoretical frameworks have been proposed to explain integration outcomes, most remain at the conceptual level, lacking the precision and predictive power that mathematical formalization can provide.

The Cultural Distance Integration Model (CDIM) addresses this gap by offering a systematic approach to understanding how cultural differences between immigrant groups and host societies affect integration success. However, to move beyond descriptive analysis towards predictive modelling and evidence-based policy design, a rigorous mathematical framework is essential. This chapter presents such a formalization, transforming the theoretical insights of CDIM into a set of mathematical relationships that can be empirically tested, computationally modelled, and practically applied.

D. Rauhut, *Institutional Economics and Immigrant Integration*,
https://doi.org/10.1007/978-3-032-28361-0_5

The Need for Mathematical Formalization

The importance of mathematical modelling in integration research stems from several critical limitations in existing approaches. First, most integration theories rely on qualitative descriptions that, while insightful, cannot generate precise predictions about integration outcomes under different conditions (Alba & Nee, 2003; Portes & Zhou, 1993). Without quantitative precision, it becomes difficult to compare integration processes across different contexts, test theoretical propositions rigorously, or design optimal policy interventions.

Second, integration is inherently a multidimensional, dynamic process involving complex interactions between cultural, social, economic, and institutional factors (Berry, 1997; Bourhis et al., 1997). These interactions often exhibit nonlinear relationships, threshold effects, and emergent properties that are difficult to capture through verbal theorizing alone. Mathematical modelling provides the tools necessary to represent these complexities systematically and explore their implications.

Third, the policy relevance of integration research depends critically on its ability to inform evidence-based decision-making. Policymakers need to know not just whether cultural distance matters, but how much it matters, under what conditions, and which interventions are most cost-effective for different immigrant populations (Joppke, 2007; Goodman, 2012). Mathematical models can provide this level of precision by quantifying relationships, identifying optimal policy mixes, and predicting outcomes under various scenarios.

Theoretical Foundations and Innovations

The mathematical framework presented in this chapter builds upon established theoretical traditions in migration and integration research while introducing several key innovations. Drawing from classical assimilation theory (Gordon, 1964), segmented assimilation theory (Portes & Rumbaut, 2001), and acculturation frameworks (Berry, 2006), the model incorporates insights about the multi-generational nature of integration, the importance of context, and the bidirectional nature of cultural change.

However, the CDIM mathematical framework goes beyond existing approaches in several important ways. First, it operationalizes cultural distance as a multidimensional construct that captures civilizational differences (Huntington, 1996), value-based differences (Hofstede, 2001), and developmental differences (Inglehart & Welzel, 2005). This multi-level approach recognizes that cultural distance is not a single phenomenon but rather emerges from the interaction of different types of cultural differences.

Second, the model incorporates explicit threshold dynamics, recognizing that integration processes often exhibit nonlinear relationships where small changes in cultural distance can lead to dramatically different outcomes (Schelling, 1978). This insight has important implications for understanding why some integration processes succeed while others fail, even when initial conditions appear similar.

Third, the framework models integration as a bidirectional process where both immigrant groups and host societies adapt over time. This represents a significant departure from one-sided assimilation models and reflects growing recognition that successful integration requires mutual accommodation (Kymlicka, 2010; Modood, 2007).

The Methodological Approach and Structure

The mathematical formalization presented in this chapter follows a systematic approach that moves from basic concepts to complex dynamics. The framework begins by defining cultural distance as a composite function operating across three levels: civilizational, dimensional, and developmental. It then develops an integration success function that captures how integration outcomes vary with cultural distance, incorporating threshold effects and contextual factors.

The model subsequently explores the specific mechanisms through which cultural distance affects integration outcomes, focusing on cognitive dissonance, social coordination difficulties, and institutional incompatibilities. These mechanism-specific models provide insight into why cultural distance matters and under what conditions its effects are most pronounced.

Building on these foundations, the framework develops dynamic models that capture how integration processes unfold over time. This includes bidirectional adaptation models that account for changes in both immigrant and host society behaviour, generational models that track cultural change across generations, and gender-differentiated models that recognize how cultural distance affects men and women differently.

Finally, the framework addresses policy applications through models of threshold dynamics, policy effectiveness, and optimal policy mix determination. These models are designed to inform evidence-based policymaking by identifying which interventions are most effective under different conditions and how resources can be allocated optimally across different policy domains.

Empirical Grounding and Validation

Throughout the development of these mathematical models, particular attention has been paid to empirical grounding and validation possibilities. The framework is designed to be operationalizable using existing data sources, including cross-national surveys like the World Values Survey (Inglehart et al., 2014), Hofstede's cultural dimensions database (Hofstede et al., 2010), and various national integration outcome measures.

The mathematical relationships specified in the model generate testable hypotheses about integration outcomes, policy effectiveness, and contextual variations. These can be evaluated using both cross-sectional and longitudinal data, allowing for empirical validation and refinement of the theoretical framework.

Contributions and Implications

This mathematical formalization of CDIM makes several important contributions to integration research and policy. Theoretically, it provides a framework for understanding complex integration processes, generating precise predictions, and testing alternative hypotheses. Methodologically, it demonstrates how qualitative theoretical insights can be transformed into quantitative models suitable for empirical analysis and computational simulation.

From a policy perspective, the framework offers tools for optimizing integration policies, predicting integration outcomes under different scenarios, and allocating resources efficiently across different intervention strategies. The models can inform decisions about which immigrant populations require the most intensive support, which policy domains should be prioritized, and how interventions should be adapted to local contexts (see, e.g., Rauhut, 2020).

The framework also has broader implications for understanding cultural diversity in increasingly multicultural societies. By providing precise tools for measuring and predicting the effects of cultural differences, it can inform debates about immigration policy, multiculturalism, and social cohesion in diverse societies.

The following sections present the detailed mathematical development of these ideas, moving systematically from basic definitions through complex dynamic models to policy applications. Throughout, the emphasis is on developing models that are both theoretically rigorous and practically useful for understanding and managing integration processes in contemporary societies.

Core Mathematical Framework

Cultural Distance Function

This section creates a cultural distance score that measures how different two cultures are from each other. Cultural distance is not just one thing, but, as was discussed previously, is made up of three different types of differences that all work together.

Let *Cultural Distance* (CD) be represented as a composite function operating across three levels:

$$\mathrm{CD}_{\mathrm{total}} = f\left(\mathrm{CD}_{\mathrm{civ}}, \mathrm{CD}_{\mathrm{dim}}, \mathrm{CD}_{\mathrm{dev}}, I\right) \tag{5.1}$$

where $\mathrm{CD}_{\mathrm{civ}}$ represents how different the civilizations are (think Western vs. Islamic vs. Confucian cultures), $\mathrm{CD}_{\mathrm{dim}}$ represents differences in cultural values (like how much people value individualism vs. collectivism), $\mathrm{CD}_{\mathrm{dev}}$ represents differences in societal development levels (traditional vs. modern values), and I is how these three types of distance interact and amplify each other. This relationship can be expressed in the specific formulation:

$$\begin{aligned}\mathrm{CD}_{\mathrm{total}} &= \alpha_1 \mathrm{CD}_{\mathrm{civ}} + \alpha_2 \mathrm{CD}_{\mathrm{dim}} + \alpha_3 \mathrm{CD}_{\mathrm{dev}} + \beta_1\left(\mathrm{CD}_{\mathrm{civ}} \times \mathrm{CD}_{\mathrm{dim}}\right) \\ &\quad + \beta_2\left(\mathrm{CD}_{\mathrm{civ}} \times \mathrm{CD}_{\mathrm{dev}}\right) + \beta_3\left(\mathrm{CD}_{\mathrm{dim}} \times \mathrm{CD}_{\mathrm{dev}}\right) \\ &\quad + \gamma\left(\mathrm{CD}_{\mathrm{civ}} \times \mathrm{CD}_{\mathrm{dim}} \times \mathrm{CD}_{\mathrm{dev}}\right)\end{aligned} \tag{5.2}$$

This equation shows that the total cultural distance is calculated by: (1) adding up the three individual distance types (the α terms), (2) adding the effects when two types interact (the β terms, i.e., like how civilizational differences might make value differences worse), and (3) adding the effect when all three interact together (the γ term). The Greek letters (α, β, γ) are weights that determine how important each component is.

Integration Success Function

This section predicts how successful integration will be based on the cultural distance calculated above. Integration success, *IS*, drops off in stages as cultural distance increases: first gradually, then rapidly, then it becomes nearly impossible. Integration Success as a threshold function:

$$\mathrm{IS}\left(\mathrm{CD}_{\mathrm{total}}\right)=\left\{\begin{array}{c}\mathrm{IS}_{\max}\times\left(1-\delta_1\mathrm{CD}_{\mathrm{total}}\right),\ \text{if}\,\mathrm{CD}_{\mathrm{total}}\leq T_1\\ \mathrm{IS}_{\max}\times\mathrm{e}^{\left(1-\delta_2\mathrm{CD}_{\mathrm{total}}\right)},\text{if}\,T_1<\mathrm{CD}_{\mathrm{total}}\leq T_2\\ \mathrm{IS}_{\min},\ \text{if}\,\mathrm{CD}_{\mathrm{total}}>T_2\end{array}\right\} \tag{5.3}$$

This threshold function contains three different zones with threshold points, T_1 and T_2, where integration difficulty jumps to the next level:

- Zone 1 ($\mathrm{CD}_{\mathrm{total}} \leq T_1$): *Manageable differences*, i.e., integration success decreases slowly and linearly
- Zone 2 ($T_1 < \mathrm{CD}_{\mathrm{total}} \leq T_2$): *Challenging differences*, i.e., integration success drops off exponentially (much faster)
- Zone 3 ($\mathrm{CD}_{\mathrm{total}} > T_2$): *Overwhelming differences*, i.e., integration success is minimal

Three-Level Distance Calculations

This section explains how to actually calculate each of the three types of cultural distance. The civilization distance, $\mathrm{CD}_{\mathrm{civ}}$, dimensional distance, $\mathrm{CD}_{\mathrm{dim}}$, and development distance, $\mathrm{CD}_{\mathrm{dev}}$, operate, as discussed earlier, at three different levels. The civilization distance expresses how different the fundamental worldviews and social systems are between cultures. This can be formulated in a simple way as:

$$\mathrm{CD}_{\mathrm{civ}}=\left\{\begin{array}{c}0,\text{if same civilization}\\ 1,\text{if different civilizations}\end{array}\right\} \tag{5.4}$$

A more sophisticated formulation of civilization distance in how different the fundamental worldviews and social systems are between cultures can be expressed as:

$$CD_{civ} = \sum_i w_i \left| Civ_{origin_i} - Civ_{host_i} \right| \tag{5.5}$$

where i is an index that runs through different civilizational dimensions or aspects, and w_i is the weight assigned to each civilizational dimension i. It represents how important that particular aspect is in determining overall civilizational distance. What the civilizational dimensions (i) might include could be religious or spiritual systems, authority structures and governance, family organization patterns, economic systems and values, legal traditions, social hierarchy concepts, etc.

As an example, if the Western civilization should be compared to another civilization, the measure of differences in religious systems would be $|\mathrm{Civ}_{\mathrm{origin},\,1} - \mathrm{Civ}_{\mathrm{host},\,1}|$ and the measure in difference in authority structures would be $|\mathrm{Civ}_{\mathrm{origin},\,2} - \mathrm{Civ}_{\mathrm{host},\,2}|$. Each difference gets multiplied by its weight (w_i) to show how much that aspect matters. Then all weighted differences are summed up (Σ) to get the total civilizational distance. What the equation is saying is add up all the weighted differences across every important aspect of civilization to get the total civilizational distance.

The dimensional distance focuses on differences in cultural values using Hofstede's framework. This includes aspects such as individualism vs. collectivism, power distance, uncertainty avoidance, etc.

$$\mathrm{CD}_{\mathrm{dim}} = \left(\frac{\left(\frac{1}{6}\right) \times \sum_j \left| D_j \mathrm{origin} - D_j \mathrm{host} \right|}{100} \right) \tag{5.6}$$

where j is an index that runs through Hofstede's six cultural dimensions (1, 2, 3, 4, 5, 6), and D_j represents the score on Hofstede dimension j. Each country gets a numerical score (typically 0–100) for each of Hofstede's cultural dimensions. What the six Hofstede dimensions (j) are:

- $j = 1$: Power Distance (how much hierarchy/inequality people accept)
- $j = 2$: Individualism vs. Collectivism (focus on individual vs. group)
- $j = 3$: Masculinity vs. Femininity (competitive vs. cooperative values)
- $j = 4$: Uncertainty Avoidance (comfort with ambiguity and risk)
- $j = 5$: Long-term vs. Short-term Orientation (future vs. present focus)
- $j = 6$: Indulgence vs. Restraint (gratification vs. social norms control)

What this equation does is to measure the absolute difference between origin and host country on each of the six Hofstede dimensions. Since Hofstede scores go 0–100, it divides by 100 to normalize. Moreover, it measures the averages across all six dimensions. Final result is between 0 and 1, where 0 = identical cultures, 1 = maximally different cultures.

The development distance measures how different societies are in terms of their development stage using the Inglehart-Welzel World Values Survey framework.

$$CD_{dev} = \frac{\sqrt{\left[\left(TS_{origin} - TS_{host}\right)^2 + \left(SE_{origin} - SE_{host}\right)^2\right]}}{\sqrt{2}} \tag{5.7}$$

where TS represents Traditional vs. Secular-rational values and SE represents Survival vs. Self-expression values. This equation calculates the distance between two points in 2D space (analogous to measuring the distance between two cities on a map). Division by $\sqrt{2}$ ensures the result stays between 0 and 1.

Mechanism-Specific Models

This section models the specific psychological and social processes that make integration difficult. The earlier theoretical discussion identified three such processes: cognitive dissonance mechanisms, social coordination difficulty, and institutional incompatibility.

Cognitive Dissonance Mechanisms

This model captures the mental stress people feel when encountering very different ways of thinking and acting.

$$\begin{aligned}\text{Cognitive dissonance} = {} & \kappa_1 \times CD_{civ}^2 + \kappa_2 \times \max\left(CD_{dim} \bullet \text{dimensions}\right) \\ & + \kappa_3 \times CD_{dev}\end{aligned} \tag{5.8}$$

where κ_1, κ_2, and κ_3 are numerical weights that determine how much each type of cultural distance contributes to cognitive dissonance. κ_1 is a weight for civilizational distance effects, which multiplies the squared civilizational distance. The squaring means civilizational differences have amplified psychological impact. κ_2 is a weight for the worst cultural dimension difference, which multiplies whichever Hofstede dimension shows the biggest gap. The model assumes the most extreme difference causes the most stress. κ_3 is a weight for developmental distance effects, which multiplies the developmental distance (traditional vs. modern values). It is a linear effect (no squaring).

The model is saying that civilizational differences (κ_1) might cause more cognitive dissonance per unit of distance than developmental differences (κ_3), and that the single worst cultural dimension mismatch (κ_2) might be more psychologically difficult than the average across all dimensions. Three conclusions can be made: civilizational differences create squared effects (much worse impact), the worst single cultural dimension difference matters most, and developmental differences add linear stress.

Social Coordination Difficulty

The social coordination difficulty aspect captures how hard it is for people from different cultures to work together and coordinate activities. The social coordination difficulty, SCD, can be expressed as:

$$SCD = \lambda_1 \times \left(CD_{dim}\right)^2 + \lambda_2 \times CD_{dev} + ND \tag{5.9}$$

where ND represents how connected the community is; network density can amplify developmental differences. λ_1 is a weight for cultural dimension distance effects, which multiplies the squared cultural dimension distance. The squaring means that coordination problems grow exponentially as cultural value differences increase. Small cultural differences might cause minor coordination issues, but large differences create major problems. λ_2 is a weight for the interaction between developmental distance and network density, which multiplies the combined effect of developmental differences *and* how connected the community is. This captures how network structure can amplify coordination problems when there are developmental gaps.

The model suggests that (a) cultural value differences (like individualism vs. collectivism) make coordination exponentially harder; it is not just twice as hard when differences are twice as big; the challenges increase exponentially. (b) Developmental differences interact with how connected people are in the community. In a tight-knit community (high network density), developmental gaps might create more coordination problems because everyone interacts with everyone else frequently. The conclusion is that cultural value differences create squared difficulties.

Institutional Incompatibility

This aspect captures how well different cultural approaches to authority, law, and social organization work together. Institutional incompatibility, *II*, can be expressed as:

$$II = \mu_1 \times \mathrm{CD}_{\mathrm{civ}} + \mu_2 \times \left|\mathrm{PD}_{\mathrm{gap}}\right| + \mu_3 \times \left|\mathrm{IC}_{\mathrm{gap}}\right| + \mu_4 \times \mathrm{CD}_{\mathrm{dev}} \tag{5.10}$$

where μ_1, μ_2, μ_3, and μ_4 are numerical weights that determine how much each factor contributes to institutional incompatibility. The $\mathrm{PD}_{\mathrm{gap}}$ is the difference between origin and host country on Hofstede's 'Power Distance' dimension, and it measures how much people accept hierarchy and inequality in society. The $\mathrm{PD}_{\mathrm{gap}}$ shows the absolute difference between the power distance in the country of origin and host country: $| \mathrm{PD}_{\mathrm{gap}} | = | \mathrm{PD}_{\mathrm{origin}} - \mathrm{PD}_{\mathrm{host}} |$. The $\mathrm{IC}_{\mathrm{gap}}$ is the difference between origin and host country on Hofstede's 'Individualism vs. Collectivism' dimension. This measures whether people focus on individual rights/responsibilities vs. group harmony/obligations. The $\mathrm{IC}_{\mathrm{gap}}$ also shows the absolute difference between country of origin and host country for this aspect.

The different components catch different aspects of the institutional incompatibility. $\mu_1 \times \mathrm{CD}_{\mathrm{civ}}$ controls for how civilizational differences affect institutional compatibility, $\mu_2 \times | \mathrm{PD}_{\mathrm{gap}} |$ controls for how differences in hierarchy acceptance affect institutional compatibility, $\mu_3 \times | \mathrm{IC}_{\mathrm{gap}} |$ controls for how differences in individual vs. group orientation affect institutional compatibility, and, finally, $\mu_4 \times \mathrm{CD}_{\mathrm{dev}}$ controls for how developmental differences affect institutional compatibility. The model treats Power Distance and Individualism-Collectivism as especially important for institutional compatibility because Power Distance affects how people expect legal systems, government, and organizations to work, and Individualism-Collectivism affects expectations about individual rights vs. collective responsibilities in institutions.

The conclusion is that civilizational differences matter directly, the *Power Distance* gap (how much hierarchy people expect) is crucial, the *Individualism-Collectivism* gap is crucial, and the developmental differences affect institutional compatibility.

Bidirectional Adaptation Model

The premise for the bidirectional adaptation model is that integration is not just immigrants adapting; host societies adapt too, and both processes happen over time. This section will formulate an immigrant adaptation function, a host society adaptation function, and a function for combined integration success.

Immigrant Adaptation Function

Immigrant adaptation, IA, can be expressed as:

$$IA(t) = IA_{max} \times \left(1 - e^{(-r_1 t)}\right) \times \left(\frac{1 - CD_{total}}{CD_{max}}\right) \tag{5.11}$$

where IA(t) represents how well immigrants have adapted at time t; the (t) means this value changes over time. It could be measured as a percentage or score (e.g., 0–1, where 1 = fully adapted). r_1 is a rate parameter for immigrant adaptation. This determines how fast immigrants adapt over time (higher r_1 means faster adaptation rate; lower r_1 means slower adaptation rate).

The subscript "1" distinguishes it from r_2 (which is used for host society adaptation rate in another equation below).

The equation components can be broken down. IA_{max} is the maximum possible adaptation level for immigrants. The $(1 - e^{(-r_1 t)})$ shows the learning curve component, which creates an S-shaped adaptation curve over time. It starts at 0 when t = 0 and approaches 1 as t increases. The $e^{(-r_1 t)}$ term gets smaller as time passes, so $(1 - e^{(-r_1 t)})$ gets larger. This models how adaptation is fast at first, then slows down as you approach your maximum. The cultural penalty distance is $(1 - CD_{total}/CD_{max})$. This reduces maximum adaptation based on how large the cultural distance is. If $CD_{total} = 0$ (no cultural distance), this equals 1 (no penalty); if $CD_{total} = CD_{max}$ (maximum cultural distance), this equals 0 (adaptation nearly impossible).

The full equation means that immigrant adaptation follows a learning curve over time, but the final level they can reach depends on how big the cultural gap is. Even with unlimited time, larger cultural distances mean lower maximum adaptation is possible.

Host Society Adaptation Function

The Host Society Adaptation Function, HSA, can be expressed as:

$$\mathrm{HSA}(t) = \mathrm{HSA}_{\max} \times \left(1 - e^{(-r_2 t)}\right) \times \mathrm{PS}(t) \times \mathrm{IF} \quad (5.12)$$

where HSA(t) represents how well the host society has adapted at time t; the (t) means this value changes over time. It could be measured as a percentage or score (e.g., 0–1, where 1 is fully adapted). r_2 is a rate parameter for host society adaptation, and it determines how fast immigrants adapt over time (higher r_2 is a faster adaptation rate; lower r_2 is a slower adaptation rate). PS(t) is the level of political support for integration at time t, which measures how much the political system and leadership support immigrant integration. It is a function of time (t) because political support can change over time, and it could be measured as a scale (e.g., 0–1, where 1 = strong political support). IF controls for institutional flexibility, i.e., how adaptable the host society's institutions are. This measures how easily institutions can accommodate cultural differences. Unlike PS, this does not have (t) as it is treated as more stable over time. IF could be measured as a scale (e.g., 0–1, where 1 is highly flexible institutions).

The conclusion is that host society adaptation (HSA) depends on both political will *and* institutional capacity. Even if there is political support for integration, rigid institutions limit how much the host society can actually adapt. Conversely, flexible institutions will not help much without political support to use that flexibility. The model suggests that successful integration requires *both* political backing *and* institutional systems that can bend to accommodate cultural differences.

Combined Integration Success

The combined integration success function can be expressed in the following way:

$$\mathrm{IS}_{\mathrm{total}}(t) = f\left(\mathrm{IA}(t), \mathrm{HSA}(t)\right) = k_1 \times \mathrm{IA}(t) + k_2 \times \mathrm{HSA}(t) + k_3\left(\mathrm{IA}(t) \times \mathrm{HSA}(t)\right) \quad (5.13)$$

where k_1 is a weight for immigrant adaptation effects. This determines how much immigrant adaptation alone contributes to total integration success; the higher k_1 means immigrant adaptation is more important for overall success. k_2 is a weight for host society adaptation effects. This determines how much host society adaptation alone contributes to total integration success; the higher k_2 means host society adaptation is more important for overall success. k_3 is a weight for the synergy/interaction effect. This multiplies the combined effect when *both* immigrant and host society adapt simultaneously, and it captures the idea that integration works best when both sides adapt together. The interaction term $\mathrm{IA}(t) \times \mathrm{HSA}(t)$ represents synergy, i.e., the total effect is greater than the sum of parts.

The model suggests three pathways to integration success: (1) a one-way adaptation where immigrants adapt (k_1 term); (2) a one-way adaptation where the host society adapts (k_2 term); and (3) a mutual adaptation where both sides adapt together, creating synergy (k_3 term). The k_3 term is crucial: it says that integration works much better when it is bidirectional rather than one-sided. When both immigrants and host society make efforts to adapt, the result is more than just adding their individual contributions together.

Threshold Dynamics

The premise on which the integration threshold dynamics is built is that the thresholds depend on circumstances. In other words, the threshold points where integration becomes much harder are not fixed. Two types of threshold models can be identified, and they will be discussed now.

Dynamic Threshold Model

A simple dynamic threshold model can be expressed in the following way:

$$\begin{aligned} T_1(\text{context}) &= T_1\text{base} + \varphi_1 \times \text{EO} + \varphi_2 \times \text{IF} + \varphi_3 \times \text{PS} \\ T_2(\text{context}) &= T_2\text{base} + \psi_1 \times \text{EO} + \psi_2 \times \text{IF} + \psi_3 \times \text{PS} \end{aligned} \tag{5.14}$$

T_1(context) and T_2(context) represent dynamic threshold values that change based on context. T_1 is the first threshold where integration difficulty jumps from ‘manageable’ to ‘challenging’, and T_2 is the second threshold where integration difficulty jumps from ‘challenging’ to ‘nearly impossible’. The ‘(context)’ means these thresholds are not fixed but shift based on circumstances. T_1 base and T_2 base are baseline threshold values, i.e., starting points for the thresholds under neutral conditions. φ (phi) are the weighting parameters for the first threshold (T_1), where φ_1 is how much economic opportunity affects the first threshold, φ_2 how much institutional flexibility affects the first threshold, and φ_3 how much political support affects the first threshold. ψ (psi) are the weighting parameters for the second threshold (T_2), where ψ_1 is how much economic opportunity affects the second threshold, ψ_2 how much institutional flexibility affects the second threshold, and ψ_3 how much political support affects the second threshold. EO represents the level of economic opportunities available. This measures things like job availability and wage levels, economic growth rate, unemployment rates, access to entrepreneurship, economic mobility prospects, labour market openness to immigrants, etc.

Conceptually, this can lead to two different outcomes. During good times (high economic opportunity, flexible institutions, political support), both T_1 and T_2 increase (shift upward). This means larger cultural distances become manageable and integration can succeed even with bigger cultural gaps. In short, during economic booms, even culturally distant groups integrate better. During bad times (economic recession, rigid institutions, political backlash), both T_1 and T_2 decrease (shift downward). This means even smaller cultural distances become problematic and integration becomes difficult even for culturally similar groups. In short, during recessions, even small cultural differences can lead to conflict. The key insight here is that the same cultural distance can lead to integration success or failure depending on the broader context. A cultural distance that works fine during prosperous times might become a major barrier during economic hardship or political tension.

Domain-Specific Thresholds

It is important to control for how flexible a domain is in accommodating differences, and how culturally important that domain is to people's identity. This can be expressed as:

$$T_{\text{domain},i} = T_{\text{base}} \times \text{DF}_i \times \text{CC}_i \tag{5.15}$$

where $T_{\text{domain},i}$ represents the cultural distance threshold for a specific life domain i. Different domains (work, education, politics, etc.) have different tolerance levels for cultural differences. *i* represents different areas of social life where integration happens. Examples of domains (i) are, e.g., ***economic domain*** (workplace, business, employment), ***educational domain*** (schools, universities, learning institutions), ***legal domain*** (courts, law enforcement, legal procedures), ***political domain*** (voting, civic participation, government), ***social domain*** (friendships, community groups, social activities), and ***religious domain*** (worship, spiritual practices). The T_{base} represents the base threshold value, i.e., the starting point or reference threshold before domain-specific adjustments. The same baseline is applied across all domains.

DF*i* is how flexible domain *i* is to cultural differences, i.e., how accommodating each specific domain is. The scale is typically 0 to 1+ (where 1 is normal flexibility, >1 is high flexibility, <1 is low flexibility). Some examples of domain flexibility can be found: (1) the economic domain often shows high flexibility (businesses adapt to diverse workers/customers); (2) the legal domain often shows low flexibility (laws apply equally, limited cultural accommodation); and (3) the educational domain shows a medium flexibility (some accommodation but core curriculum remains).

How culturally important domain *i* is, cultural centrality for the domain *i* (*CCi*), measures how central this domain is to cultural identity. The scale typically ranges from 0 to 1+ (where higher values are more culturally central). Among cultural centrality domains, some examples can be found: (1) the Religious domain often has high centrality (core to cultural identity), (2) the Economic domain often has lower centrality (more pragmatic, less identity-defining), and (3) the Family/social domain often has high centrality (fundamental to cultural values).

What the equation means is that each life domain has its own tolerance threshold for cultural differences. This threshold depends on how flexible that domain is in accommodating differences, and how culturally important that domain is to people's identity.

Models for Generations, Gender, and Class

Cultural distances are assumed to shrink over generations as immigrant families become more similar to the host society. This is expressed as:

$$\text{CD}_{\text{gen}}(n) = \text{CD}_{\text{initial}} \times \rho^{n} + \left(1-\rho^{n}\right) \times \text{CD}_{\text{equilibrium}} \tag{5.16}$$

where $CD_{gen}(n)$ is the cultural distance between the immigrant group and host society at generation n. Generation 0 is the first-generation immigrants, generation 1 is the second-generation immigrants, generation 2 is the grandchildren of the original immigrants, etc. $CD_{initial}$ is the cultural distance of the first-generation immigrants ($n = 0$), i.e., how culturally different the original immigrants were from the host society. This represents the starting point of the process. @ is a cultural persistence parameter, which determines how much of the original culture persists across generations. It ranges $0 < \rho < 1$; the higher ρ means that culture persists more strongly across generations, and the lower ρ means culture changes more rapidly across generations. The long-term equilibrium cultural distance is expressed as $CD_{equilibrium}$, and it is the cultural distance that the immigrant group will eventually reach after many generations. Some cultural differences typically remain permanently, which means that $CD_{equilibrium}$ is usually never zero. It represents the 'settled' level of cultural difference in the long run.

The equation works the following way: the term ρ^n gets smaller with each generation. For example, Generation 0: $\rho^0 = 1$ (full original culture); Generation 1: $\rho^1 = \rho$ (some culture lost); Generation 2: ρ^2 (more culture lost); etc. As n increases, ρ^n approaches 0. Each generation (n) has smaller cultural distance than the previous one. The term $(1 - \rho^n)$ gets larger with each generation. Together, this represents a movement towards the equilibrium level.

Conceptually, this means that each generation is a blend between the original immigrant culture (weighted by ρ^n) and the long-term equilibrium culture (weighted by $1 - \rho^n$). Over time, the influence of the original culture fades while the equilibrium influence grows, but some cultural distance typically remains permanently, especially if the CD was huge for the first-generation immigrants.

Integration Success Across Generations

Looking only at the first generation of immigrants can give a misleading impression because initial challenges like language barriers, economic adjustment, or legal status often obscure long-term patterns. By examining the experiences of their children and grandchildren, it is possible to identify whether barriers to education, employment, civic participation, and social mobility persist or diminish. In other words, it is a lens for measuring whether opportunity is expanding or stagnating across time. This process can be expressed as:

$$IS_{gen}(n) = IS(CD_{gen}(n)) \times GA_n \tag{5.17}$$

where $IS_{gen}(n)$ shows the integration success for generation n, i.e., how successful integration is for the nth generation. This is the final integration success score after accounting for both cultural distance and generational advantages. $IS(CD_{gen}(n))$ is an integration success function applied to the cultural distance of generation n, which takes the cultural distance of generation n and runs it through the integration success function. Please keep in mind that the IS function shows how integration success decreases as cultural distance increases. Since $CD_{gen}(n)$ gets smaller with each generation, $IS(CD_{gen}(n))$ gets larger, i.e., better integration is achieved. GAn represents the additional advantages that generation n has beyond just cultural distance. This advantage represents all the non-cultural advantages that later generations accumulate. It typically increases with each generation, so later generations have more advantages.

Generational advantages can be described the following way. The first generation ($n = 0$) has limited language skills, fewer social networks, less familiarity with institutions, and their foreign credentials may not be recognized. The second generation has good language fluency, local education and credentials, better understanding of social norms, and larger social networks including host society members. The third generation ($n = 2$) has fully native language and cultural competence, established professional and social networks, complete familiarity with institutions, and may have family connections in mainstream society.

What the equation means is that integration success for each generation depends on two factors. The first is cultural distance effects: How much their remaining cultural differences hurt integration? The second is generational advantages: How much their accumulated advantages (language, networks, knowledge) help integration? Even if cultural distance only improves modestly between generations, integration success can improve dramatically because of these accumulated advantages. A third-generation person might have only slightly less cultural distance than a second-generation person, but much better integration outcomes due to their additional advantages.

Gender-Differentiated Integration Model

The premise for gender-differentiated integration is that men and women from the same cultural background often experience systematically different integration trajectories due to cultural norms about gender roles, expectations, and opportunities that they bring from their origin countries. Cultural distance affects men and women differently depending on origin country gender norms. This can be expressed as:

$$\mathrm{CD}_{\mathrm{gender}}\left(m/f,n\right)=\mathrm{CD}_{\mathrm{gen}}\left(n\right)\times\mathrm{GN}_{\mathrm{modifier}}\left(m/f\right)\times\mathrm{GD}_{\mathrm{gap}} \tag{5.18}$$

where $\mathrm{CD}_{\mathrm{gender}}(m/f,n)$ represents the effective cultural distance for males (m) or females (f) at generation n. $\mathrm{CD}_{\mathrm{gen}}(n)$ is the baseline cultural distance at generation n from Eq. (5.16). $\mathrm{GN}_{\mathrm{modifier}}(m/f)$ is the gender norm modifier that adjusts cultural distance based on origin country gender expectations. $\mathrm{GD}_{\mathrm{gap}}$ represents the gender development gap between origin and host countries. The gender norm modifier can be formulated as:

$$GN_{modifier}\left(m/f\right)=1+\alpha_{gender}\times\left|GE_{origin}-GE_{host}\right|\times GRR \tag{5.19}$$

where $\mathrm{GE}_{\mathrm{origin}}$ and $\mathrm{GE}_{\mathrm{host}}$ represent gender equality indices in origin and host countries, respectively, and Gender Role Rigidity, GRR, measures how strictly defined gender roles are in the origin culture. α_{gender} is a weighting parameter for gender effects.

Different life domains present varying gender-specific integration challenges:

$$\mathrm{IS}_{\mathrm{gender}}\left(\mathrm{domain},m/f,n\right)=\mathrm{IS}_{\mathrm{gen}}\left(n\right)\times\mathrm{GF}_{\mathrm{domain}}\left(m/f\right)\times\mathrm{GC}_{\mathrm{domain}} \tag{5.20}$$

where $\mathrm{GF}_{\mathrm{domain}}(m/f)$ represents gender-specific facilitation factors for each domain, and $\mathrm{GC}_{\mathrm{domain}}$ represents gender-specific constraints in each domain. Domain-specific gender factors include economic domain (women may face additional barriers in male-dominated professions, traditional gender roles may limit women's workforce participation, and credential recognition may differ by gender in certain fields), educational domain (cultural restrictions on women's education from origin country, different educational expectations for sons vs. daughters, and adult education access may be gendered), and social domain (gender-segregated social networks in some cultures, different mobility and social participation norms, and marriage and family formation pattern differences).

Gender integration patterns often shift dramatically across generations:

$$\mathrm{GI}_{\mathrm{evolution}}(n) = \mathrm{GI}_{\mathrm{initial}} \times \theta^n + \left(1 - \theta^n\right) \times \mathrm{GI}_{\mathrm{host\_}norm} \tag{5.21}$$

where $\mathrm{GI}_{\mathrm{evolution}}(n)$ represents gender integration patterns at generation n, $\mathrm{GI}_{\mathrm{initial}}$ represents initial gender role patterns from origin culture, θ (theta) is the gender cultural persistence parameter, and $\mathrm{GI}_{\mathrm{host\_norm}}$ represents host society gender norms. This equation captures how first-generation women may maintain traditional gender roles even if host society is more egalitarian, second-generation women often experience conflict between family expectations and host society opportunities, and third-generation patterns typically converge towards host society norms, but some differences may persist.

In conclusion, this gender-differentiated model reveals several key insights. The first is that integration is asymmetric. Men and women from the same cultural background may have vastly different integration trajectories. A second insight relates to domain specificity. Gender effects vary significantly across life domains (economic, social, educational). A third insight is that gender integration patterns do not simply linearize across generations but may involve conflict and negotiation. The model suggests that ignoring gender dimensions can lead to both theoretical misspecification and policy ineffectiveness, as it fails to capture roughly half the complexity of the integration process.

Class-Differentiated Integration Model

The premise for class-differentiated integration is that immigrants from different socioeconomic backgrounds experience systematically different integration trajectories, even when originating from the same cultural context. Cultural distance interacts with class position to create distinct integration pathways, as economic resources, social capital, and cultural capital provide varying degrees of buffer against cultural distance effects.

Cultural distance affects different socioeconomic groups differently depending on their access to resources that can mitigate cultural barriers. This can be expressed as:

$$\mathrm{CD}_{\mathrm{class}}\left(c,n\right)=\mathrm{CD}_{\mathrm{gen}}\left(n\right)\times\mathrm{CR}_{\mathrm{modifier}}\left(c\right)\times\mathrm{SES}_{\mathrm{gap}} \quad (5.22)$$

where $\mathrm{CD}_{\mathrm{class}}(c,n)$ represents the effective cultural distance for socioeconomic class c at generation n, $\mathrm{CD}_{\mathrm{gen}}(n)$ is the baseline cultural distance at generation n from Eq. (5.16), $\mathrm{CR}_{\mathrm{modifier}}(c)$ is the class resource modifier that adjusts cultural distance based on available resources, and $\mathrm{SES}_{\mathrm{gap}}$ represents the socioeconomic status gap between origin and host countries. The class resource modifier can be formulated as:

$$\mathrm{CR}_{\mathrm{modifier}}\left(c\right)=1-\beta_{\mathrm{econ}}\times\mathrm{EC}_{\mathrm{c}}-\beta_{\mathrm{social}}\times\mathrm{SC}_{\mathrm{c}}-\beta_{\mathrm{cultural}}\times\mathrm{CC}_{\mathrm{c}}+\beta_{\mathrm{rigid}}\times\mathrm{CR}_{\mathrm{c}} \quad (5.23)$$

where EC_{c} represents economic capital available to class c (income, wealth, financial resources), SC_{c} represents social capital available to class c (networks, connections, institutional access), CC_{c} represents cultural capital available to class c (education, language skills, cultural knowledge), and CR_{c} represents cultural rigidity constraints that may increase with higher class position in origin country.

The β parameters weight the different capital effects, where β_{econ}, β_{social}, and $\beta_{\mathrm{cultural}}$ are typically positive (resources reduce effective cultural distance), while β_{rigid} may be positive (higher origin-country status may increase resistance to adaptation).

Different life domains present varying class-specific integration challenges:

$$\mathrm{IS}_{\mathrm{class}}\left(\mathrm{domain},c,n\right)=\mathrm{IS}_{\mathrm{gen}}\left(n\right)\times\mathrm{CF}_{\mathrm{domain}}\left(c\right)\times\mathrm{CB}_{\mathrm{domain}}\left(c\right)\times\mathrm{CP}_{\mathrm{domain}}\left(c\right) \quad (5.24)$$

where $\mathrm{CF}_{\mathrm{domain}}(c)$ represents class-specific facilitation factors for each domain, $\mathrm{CB}_{\mathrm{domain}}(c)$ represents class-specific barriers in each domain, and $\mathrm{CP}_{\mathrm{domain}}(c)$ represents class-specific privileges or penalties in each domain. What the domain-specific class factors include is displayed in Table 5.1.

Class position often shifts across generations, creating complex interactions between social mobility and cultural adaptation:

$$\mathrm{CM}_{\mathrm{evolution}}\left(n\right)=\mathrm{CM}_{\mathrm{initial}}\times\rho_{\mathrm{class}^{n}}+\left(1-\rho_{\mathrm{class}^{n}}\right)\times\mathrm{CM}_{\mathrm{host\ distribution}}\times M_{\mathrm{factor}}\left(n\right) \quad (5.25)$$

Table 5.1 Class-specific integration challenges for different life domains

	Economic domain	*Educational domain*	*Social domain*
Upper class	May face credential recognition barriers but have resources for retraining; existing wealth provides buffer during transition periods; professional networks may be limited initially but expandable through elite institutions	Can afford private schools and tutoring to overcome cultural/ language gaps; has cultural capital to navigate elite educational institutions; may maintain parallel cultural education	Can access exclusive social networks but may face exclusion from established elite circles; maintains transnational social connections; cultural distance may be more pronounced in elite social settings
Middle class	Faces credential recognition challenges with limited financial buffer; may experience downward mobility initially; professional skills may transfer but institutional knowledge lacking	Relies on public education system; may struggle with competing cultural expectations; limited resources for supplementary education	Seeks integration into mainstream middle-class social networks; may experience status anxiety and identity conflicts; balances origin and host cultural expectations
Working class	May find manual labour opportunities with fewer credential barriers; faces language barriers in workplace advancement; limited resources for skill upgrading or retraining	Faces multiple barriers including economic constraints on education; may prioritize immediate economic needs over educational investment; limited cultural capital for educational navigation	May form insular community networks; faces fewer expectations for cultural assimilation in some contexts; economic constraints limit social participation opportunities

Source: Own elaboration

where $\text{CM}_{\text{evolution}}(n)$ represents class mobility patterns at generation n, $\text{CM}_{\text{initial}}$ represents the initial class position in the origin-country context, ρ_{class} is the class persistence parameter across generations, $\text{CM}_{\text{host\_distribution}}$ represents the class distribution opportunities in the host society, and $M_{\text{factor}}(n)$ represents mobility factors that change across generations.

The mobility factor can be decomposed as:

$$M_{\text{factor}}(n) = M_{\text{structural}} \times M_{\text{cultural}}(n) \times M_{\text{discrimination}}(n) \tag{5.26}$$

where $M_{\text{structural}}$ represents structural mobility opportunities in the host society, $M_{\text{cultural}}(n)$ represents cultural adaptation advantages that accumulate across generations, and $M_{\text{discrimination}}(n)$ represents discrimination effects that may vary by generation and class position.

Integration success varies not only by generation but by the interaction between class position and cultural distance:

$$\text{IS}_{\text{class gen}}(c,n) = \text{IS}_{\text{baseline}}(n) \times \left[1 + \gamma_{\text{up}} \times I_{\text{up}}(c,n) - \gamma_{\text{down}} \times I_{\text{downward}}(c,n)\right] \times \text{CD}_{\text{adjustment}}(c,n) \tag{5.27}$$

where $\text{IS}_{\text{baseline}}(n)$ is the baseline integration success for generation n, $I_{\text{upward}}(c,n)$ represents upward mobility effects for class c at generation n, $I_{\text{downward}}(c,n)$ represents downward mobility effects, and $\text{CD}_{\text{adjustment}}(c,n)$ captures how class position modifies cultural distance effects.

The cultural distance adjustment can be specified as:

$$\text{CD}_{\text{adjustment}}(c,n) = 1 - \alpha_{\text{buffer}} \times \text{Resource}_{\text{buffer}}(c,n) + \alpha_{\text{rigidity}} \times \text{Status}_{\text{rigidity}}(c,n) \tag{5.28}$$

where $\text{Resource}_{\text{buffer}}(c,n)$ represents accumulated resources that buffer against cultural distance effects, and $\text{Status}_{\text{rigidity}}(c,n)$ represents status-based resistance to cultural adaptation.

Integration outcomes are also influenced by interactions across class boundaries within immigrant communities:

$$\text{Cross class}_{\text{effect}} = \delta_{\text{solidarity}} \times \text{Community}_{\text{solidarity}} - \delta_{\text{stratification}} \times \text{internal}_{\text{stratification}} \tag{5.29}$$

where $\text{Community}_{\text{solidarity}}$ represents the degree to which different classes within the immigrant community support each other's integration, and $\text{Internal}_{\text{stratification}}$ represents the degree to which class divisions within the immigrant community hinder collective integration efforts.

The class-differentiated model reveals several key policy insights. One insight relates to *resource-based interventions*. Different classes require different types of support—upper-class immigrants may need credential recognition and professional networking support, middle-class immigrants may need financial bridging support during transition periods, and working-class immigrants may need basic language and skill training programmes. A second relates to *domain-specific policies.* Integration policies should be tailored not just to cultural distance but to the intersection of cultural distance and class position in specific life domains. A third has to do with *intergenerational considerations.* Policy design should account for the fact that class mobility and cultural adaptation interact across generations, potentially creating both opportunities and tensions.

This class-differentiated model demonstrates that cultural distance effects are mediated by socioeconomic resources and class position, creating distinct integration pathways that require differentiated policy responses. Ignoring class dimensions can lead to both theoretical misspecification and policy ineffectiveness, as it fails to capture how economic and social resources interact with cultural factors to shape integration outcomes.

Spatial Amplification of Cultural Distance

In order to capture the spatial amplification effects discussed previously, the mathematical structure of the CDIM must be expanded to incorporate spatial dynamics. Spatial configurations can modify cultural distance effects by influencing contact opportunities, exposure levels, and institutional engagement pathways. Thus, the effective cultural distance experienced by immigrants is not constant across locations but varies systematically with spatial distribution.

Let us denote Spatial Amplification Factor (SAF) as a scalar that modifies the total cultural distance based on residential concentration levels and the spatial heterogeneity of the area. The adjusted cultural distance becomes:

$$\mathrm{CD}_{\mathrm{spatial}} = \mathrm{CD}_{\mathrm{total}} \times \mathrm{SAF}\left(x,y,t\right) \tag{5.30}$$

Here, $\mathrm{CD}_{\mathrm{total}}$ is the composite cultural distance as previously modelled, and $\mathrm{SAF}(x,y,t)$ is a space-time dependent factor where x and y represent geographic coordinates, and t denotes time. SAF increases with the degree of cultural clustering and decreases with exposure to diverse social networks. For instance, in neighbourhoods where culturally distant groups constitute a demographic majority, and where intergroup interaction is limited, SAF increases the effective cultural distance experienced, thereby lowering integration success. Integration success then becomes:

$$IS_{spatial} = IS\left(CD_{spatial}\right) = IS_{max} \times \left(1 - \delta\left(CD_{total} \times SAF\right)\right) \tag{5.31}$$

This formulation aligns with Putnam's (2007) observations on reduced trust and civic participation in ethnically segregated areas, and accounts for the possibility that identical cultural distances have differential effects depending on spatial context. SAF can be further decomposed into elements such as enclave density, average intergroup contact probability, and institutional proximity. Such decomposition would permit policymakers and researchers to simulate how changes in residential planning or urban policy could impact integration outcomes.

The spatial component also interacts with generational adaptation. Children born into highly segregated cultural enclaves are socialized within bounded cultural systems that may reinforce origin-based norms more strongly than if they were exposed to mixed environments. Modelling intergenerational effects requires integrating SAF into the generational decay function:

$$CD_{gen_{spatial}}\left(n\right) = CD_{initial} \times \rho^{n} \times SAF_{n} + \left(1 - \rho^{n}\right) \times CD_{equilibrium} \tag{5.32}$$

This expression links cultural difference across generations to both decay and reinforcement, where $CD_{initial}$ represents the original cultural difference at generation zero, ρn reflects how cultural norms typically fade over n generations (called the generational decay function), SAF_n stands for the *spatial amplification factor*, which boosts persistence in clustered environments, and $CD_{equilibrium}$ is the level cultural norms would normally settle at over time without reinforcement.

In simpler terms, *spatial amplification* delays convergence towards this equilibrium because SAF_n keeps the original norms alive longer, especially when ρ is high. That means in tightly knit cultural enclaves, traditions stay strong even after several generations. This adjustment to the model helps predict long-term cultural dynamics more accurately, which is vital for urban planning and shaping policies in diverse communities.

Policy Intervention Model

The underlying premise for the policy intervention model is that government policies can improve integration outcomes, but their effectiveness depends on the cultural distance. This can be controlled by a policy effectiveness function and an optimal policy mix.

Policy Effectiveness Function

To model on how well a policy achieves its intended goals, it is important to formulate a policy effectiveness function to control for the result for different variables like cost, reach, and societal impact. It can be considered as a bridge between ambition and reality, and it can be expressed as:

$$PE = \sum_{i} P_i \times E_i \times \left(\frac{1 - CD_{total}}{CD_{max}} \right) \quad (5.33)$$

where the total effect of all policy interventions combined is termed Policy Effect, PE, and is the sum of all individual policy effects. This variable is the overall impact that government policies have on improving integration success. i represents different kinds of policies that can be implemented. Examples of policy types (i) are language training programmes, job training and employment assistance, cultural orientation programmes, anti-discrimination enforcement, community integration initiatives, educational support programmes, housing assistance programmes, etc.

The policy intensity or investment level for policy type i, P_i, represents how much effort or resources are put into each policy. It could be measured as funding level, programme size, or implementation intensity. Higher the P_i, the more the investment in that policy type. Language training might have high effectiveness (proven to work well). While job training programmes might have medium-high effectiveness, some awareness campaigns might have low effectiveness (limited proven impact).

The equation also contains a cultural distance modifier ($1 - CD_{total}/CD_{max}$), which reduces policy effectiveness when cultural distance is large. When $CD_{total} = 0$ there is no cultural distance, and the modifier = 1 (no reduction in effectiveness); when $CD_{total} = CD_{max}$, there is a maximum cultural distance, and modifier = 0 (policies become ineffective); and when CD_{total} is moderate, modifier is between 0 and 1.

What this equation shows is that each policy's impact is determined by (Investment Level) × (Inherent Effectiveness) × (Cultural Distance Penalty). All individual policy impacts are summed up (Σ_i) to get total policy effect. The key insight is that even the best policies with maximum funding become less effective when cultural distances are very large; all policies work better when cultural distance is smaller.

Gender-Responsive Policy Framework

Policy effectiveness must account for differential gender impacts:

$$\mathrm{PE}_{\mathrm{gender}} = \sum_i P_i \times E_i \times \mathrm{GE}_{\mathrm{factor}}\left(m/f\right) \times \left(\frac{\left(1-\mathrm{CD}_{\mathrm{gender}}\left(m/f\right)\right)}{\mathrm{CD}_{\max}}\right) \quad (5.34)$$

where $\mathrm{GE}_{\mathrm{factor}}(m/f)$ represents how each policy type affects men and women differently. Gender-responsive policies might include language training (there may be a need for childcare provisions and flexible scheduling for women), employment programmes (should address occupational segregation and credential recognition gaps), cultural orientation (must address gender role negotiations and legal rights), and social integration (may require gender-sensitive approaches to community building).

Optimal Policy Mix

The idea of an optimal policy mix is like orchestrating a symphony: each policy instrument (taxes, subsidies, regulations, education campaigns, etc.) plays a different role, and together they need to harmonize to reach your goals efficiently and effectively. Crafting an optimal policy mix is crucial because real-world challenges are rarely solved by a single policy. Societies face multiple, often competing goals, like promoting economic growth while protecting the environment, and no one-size-fits-all solution can address them all. By combining different policy instruments such as taxes, subsidies, regulations, and public education campaigns, decision-makers can tackle these goals in a balanced and strategic way.

Some policies complement each other, amplifying their overall impact. For example, language training programmes for newcomers might be far more effective when combined with job placement services and mentorship initiatives that connect immigrants with established members of the community. At the same time, relying too heavily on a single instrument, like offering legal status without providing pathways to social and economic participation, could have negative consequences, whether social, economic, or political. A thoughtful mix helps mitigate those risks.

Resource efficiency also plays a major role. With limited budgets and political capital, it is vital to allocate efforts where they will have the biggest impact. An optimal policy mix does exactly that: it ensures that you are getting the best results from the resources available. Lastly, having a diverse set of policy tools provides flexibility. As conditions change, be it due to new data, technological advancements, or economic shifts, a well-composed policy mix allows governments to adapt more nimbly.

For this study, an optimal policy mix can be expressed as follows:

$$\begin{aligned} &\text{Maximize}: IS_{total}\left(P_1, P_2, \ldots, P_n\right) \\ &\text{Subject to}: \sum_i \text{Cost}_i \times P_i \leq Budget \\ &\qquad CD_{total}\ \text{given} \end{aligned} \tag{5.35}$$

This equation represents an optimization problem, as it is trying to find the best possible policy mix. IS_{total} is the total integration success. This is what we are trying to maximize, i.e., make as large as possible, and it is the overall goal of the policy intervention. (P_1, P_2, ..., P_n) are policy variables we can control. For example, P_1 is the investment level in policy 1 (e.g., language training), P_2 is the investment level in policy 2 (e.g., job training), P_3 is the investment level in policy 3 (e.g., cultural programmes), and P_n is the investment level in policy n. These are the 'decision variables', i.e., what policymakers can choose.

The policies are subject to $\Sigma_i\ \text{Cost}_i \times P_i \leq \text{Budget}$, where Cost_i is the cost per unit of policy type i. This represents how much it costs to implement one unit of each policy. $\Sigma_i\ \text{Cost}_i \times P_i$ is the total cost of all policies combined, i.e., the sum of (cost per unit × number of units) for all policy types. *Budget* is the total available budget or resources. This is a constraint as it is not possible to spend more than this amount. CD_{total} given means that it is not possible to change the cultural distance, i.e., we must work with whatever cultural distance exists. This is a given constraint and not something we can optimize.

This optimization problem means that given a fixed budget and a specific cultural distance, the best combination of policies to maximize integration success is needed. The key insight is that the optimal policy mix depends on the cultural distance. Groups with different cultural distance profiles need different policy approaches to achieve maximum integration success within budget constraints.

Summary

This chapter introduces a mathematical model developed to systematically analyse cultural differences and their impact on the process of integration. At its foundation, the model measures cultural distance across three principal dimensions (norms, values, and behavioural patterns), offering a structured framework for examining how these differences shape interactions between immigrant communities and host societies.

A notable feature of the model is its capacity to predict integration outcomes. It identifies critical threshold points beyond which integration becomes substantially more challenging. These difficulties are not merely social in nature but arise from specific mechanisms: individuals undergoing cultural dissonance may suffer psychological strain, while institutions encounter rigidity and coordination failures as they attempt to reconcile divergent cultural expectations.

Unlike static models, this framework incorporates the principle of adaptation on both sides. Immigrant populations are not treated as immutable, nor are host societies. Instead, the model acknowledges the evolving nature of integration, wherein immigrants gradually adjust to prevailing norms, and host societies likewise transform, either in response to newcomers or through autonomous social evolution. This bidirectional dynamic is key to understanding how cultural distance can shift, lessen or even be redefined over time.

Context plays a decisive role in shaping integration trajectories. The same degree of cultural distance may produce entirely different results depending on broader societal conditions. The model emphasizes that economic stability, political support, and institutional flexibility serve as mediating influences. For example, considerable cultural difference may lead to successful integration in an economically prosperous and politically inclusive setting, whereas identical differences might cause alienation or friction in environments marked by austerity or rigidity.

Generational change is also central to the model's analytical scope. It illustrates how integration often unfolds across multiple generations, with initial cultural barriers giving way to hybrid identities and more nuanced understandings of belonging. This long-term perspective highlights that successful integration is rarely achieved through short-term initiatives alone; it requires sustained engagement across time.

Crucially, the model integrates gender considerations. It maintains that effective integration policies must be gender-aware, recognizing that men and women may experience cultural transitions in distinct ways. Gender-neutral approaches, while seemingly equitable, risk glossing over specific challenges faced by different genders and may consequently be less impactful in practice.

Spatial dimensions further refine the model's explanatory power, where individuals who settle geographically (e.g., in urban centres, peripheral towns, or culturally homogeneous enclaves) significantly influence their integration outcomes. By mapping location against cultural variables, the model sheds light on how place interacts with identity to produce diverse integration pathways.

Finally, the model is designed not merely as a tool for scholarly analysis but as a guide for policy formulation. By differentiating between cultural distance profiles and aligning these with appropriate mechanisms, it enables policymakers to craft interventions that are context-sensitive and culturally informed. One-size-fits-all solutions are inadequate in addressing such complex dynamics; this model champions nuanced, adaptable strategies instead.

The overarching insight is that cultural distance is not a single figure but a multifaceted, evolving phenomenon. It affects integration through numerous pathways, responds to social and policy influences, and requires thoughtful, context-aware engagement. By revealing these intricacies, the model equips researchers and decision-makers with the conceptual tools necessary to foster more inclusive and resilient societies.

References

Alba, R., & Nee, V. (2003). *Remaking the American mainstream: Assimilation and contemporary immigration*. Harvard University Press.

Berry, J. W. (1997). Immigration, acculturation, and adaptation. *Applied Psychology, 46*(1), 5–34. https://doi.org/10.1111/j.1464-0597.1997.tb01087.x

Berry, J. W. (2006). Acculturation: Living successfully in two cultures. *International Journal of Intercultural Relations, 29*(6), 697–712. https://doi.org/10.1016/j.ijintrel.2005.07.013

Bourhis, R. Y., Moïse, L. C., Perreault, S., & Senécal, S. (1997). Towards an interactive acculturation model: A social psychological approach. *International Journal of Psychology, 32*(6), 369–386. https://doi.org/10.1080/002075997400629

Goodman, S. W. (2012). Integration requirements for integration's sake? Identifying, categorising and comparing civic integration policies. *Journal of Ethnic and Migration Studies, 36*(5), 753–772. https://doi.org/10.1080/13691831003764300

Gordon, M. (1964). *Assimilation in American life. The role of race, religion, and national origins.* Oxford University Press.

Hofstede, G. (2001). *Culture's consequences: Comparing values, Behaviors, institutions and organizations across nations.* Sage.

Hofstede, G., Hofstede, G. J., & Minkov, M. (2010). *Cultures and organizations: Software of the mind.* McGraw-Hill.

Huntington, S. P. (1996). *The clash of civilizations and the remaking of world order.* Simon & Schuster.

Inglehart, R., Haerpfer, C., Moreno, A., Welzel, C., Kizilova, K., Diez-Medrano, J., Lagos, M., Norris, P., Ponarin, E., & Puranen, B. (2014). *World values survey: Round six - country-pooled Datafile version: www.worldvaluessurvey.org/WVSDocumentationWV6.jsp.* JD Systems Institute.

Inglehart, R. F., & Welzel, C. (2005). *Modernization, cultural change, and democracy.* Cambridge University Press.

Joppke, C. (2007). Beyond national models: Civic integration policies for immigrants in Western Europe. *West European Politics, 30*(1), 1–22. https://doi.org/10.1080/01402380601019613

Kymlicka, W. (2010). The rise and fall of multiculturalism? New debates on inclusion and accommodation in diverse societies. *International Social Science Journal, 61*(199), 97–112. https://doi.org/10.1111/j.1468-2451.2010.01750.x

Modood, T. (2007). *Multiculturalism: A Civic Idea.* Polity Press.

Portes, A., & Rumbaut, R. G. (2001). *Legacies: The story of the immigrant second generation.* University of California Press.

Portes, A., & Zhou, M. (1993). The new second generation: Segmented assimilation and its variants. *Annals of the American Academy of Political and Social Science, 530*(1), 74–96. https://doi.org/10.1177/0002716293530001006

Putnam, R. D. (2007). E Pluribus Unum: Diversity and Community in the Twenty-first Century. *Scandinavian Political Studies, 30*(2), 137–174. https://doi.org/10.1111/j.1467-9477.2007.00176.x

Rauhut, D. (2020). Integration and informal institutions. *Society, 57*(2), 211–218. https://doi.org/10.1007/s12115-020-00467-6

Schelling, T. C. (1978). *Micromotives and macrobehavior.* W.W. Norton & Company.

CHAPTER 6

Towards Precision Integration Policies

Introduction

The Cultural Distance Integration Model (CDIM), as formalized in Chap. 5, provides a rigorous framework for understanding the nonlinear relationship between cultural distance and immigrant integration outcomes. It builds upon the theoretical foundation laid in Chap. 3, which conceptualizes informal institutions, i.e., norms, values, and preferences, as central to the integration process (North, 1990; Searle, 2005; Rauhut, 2020). These informal institutions are not easily altered; they are embedded in collective memory and social practice, and their transformation often requires both incentives and constraints (Rauhut et al., 2023).

Traditional integration policies have largely operated under the assumption that standardized interventions, e.g., language training, civic orientation, and labour market access, can be uniformly applied across immigrant populations. However, the CDIM demonstrates that cultural distance creates structural constraints that cannot be overcome through linear scaling of existing programmes (Goodman, 2012; Joppke, 2007). Integration success is shaped by threshold dynamics, mechanism-specific barriers, and bidirectional adaptation processes, all of which require differentiated policy responses.

This chapter proposes a precision integration policy architecture grounded in the CDIM's mathematical logic and the theoretical role of informal institutions. It argues for targeted interventions calibrated to the

D. Rauhut, *Institutional Economics and Immigrant Integration*,
https://doi.org/10.1007/978-3-032-28361-0_6

cultural distance profile of immigrant groups, recognizing that integration is not merely a matter of resource provision but of normative negotiation. The chapter is structured around key dimensions of the CDIM: threshold-based policy architecture, mechanism-specific interventions, bidirectional adaptation, contextual calibration, generational sequencing, gender responsiveness, spatial targeting, resource optimization, and implementation feasibility.

Threshold-Based Policy Architecture

The CDIM identifies three distinct zones of cultural distance: manageable, challenging, and overwhelming. These zones correspond to threshold points (T_1 and T_2) in the integration success function, beyond which integration outcomes decline nonlinearly (see Chap. 5, Eq. 3). This threshold logic reflects the degree of divergence between informal institutions and the resulting friction in social interaction (Rauhut, 2020; see also Penninx, 2003).

In the manageable zone ($CD_{total} \leq T_1$), standard integration policies, e.g., language instruction, civic orientation, and employment support, are generally sufficient. These policies are most effective for immigrants from culturally proximate societies, such as intra-European migration or skilled migrants from liberal democracies (Alba & Nee, 2003; Mügge & van der Haar, 2016). For example, Dutch civic integration courses ('inburgering') that combine language training with basic knowledge of Dutch society have proven a paradigmatic case of civic integration (Goodman, 2014). For immigrants that are culturally relatively close, such as, e.g., EU citizens and other Western immigrants, it can be assumed that they obtain tools to a successful integration through this standardized policy.

In the challenging zone ($T_1 < CD_{total} \leq T_2$), integration difficulty increases exponentially. Immigrants from societies with moderate cultural divergence, e.g., collectivist East Asian or Latin American contexts, require multidimensional interventions. These include intensive language programmes with embedded cultural orientation, mentorship schemes linking newcomers with host society members, and structured intercultural dialogue platforms. For instance, Germany's integration courses (Integrationskurse) have evolved to include modules on gender equality, democratic values, and legal norms, reflecting the need to address deeper normative gaps (Chemin & Nagel, 2020; OECD, 2024).

In the overwhelming zone ($CD_{total} > T_2$), standard policies are largely ineffective. Immigrants from civilizationally distinct societies, e.g., conservative religious or tribal-based communities, face profound normative dissonance. Here, integration requires extended transition periods, community-based mediation, and alternative pathways that acknowledge the persistence of cultural difference.

Policy architecture must therefore be threshold-sensitive, allocating resources not by population size but by cultural distance severity. This requires diagnostic tools capable of measuring civilizational, dimensional, and developmental distance (see Chap. 5, Eqs. 1–7), and policy frameworks that respond proportionally to integration friction.

Mechanism-Specific Policy Interventions

The CDIM identifies three mechanisms through which cultural distance impedes integration: cognitive dissonance, social coordination difficulty, and institutional incompatibility (see Chap. 5, Eqs. 8–10). Each mechanism corresponds to specific psychological, social, and institutional challenges that require tailored policy responses.

Cognitive dissonance arises when immigrants encounter fundamentally different worldviews, producing psychological stress and identity conflict (Gavrilets & Richerson, 2017; Berry, 2005). This is particularly acute in cases of civilizational divergence, where religious, familial, and moral frameworks differ radically. Policies must therefore include mental health support, cultural mediation, and graduated exposure programmes.

Social coordination difficulty reflects the exponential growth of interactional friction as cultural dimension differences increase (see Chap. 5, Eq. 9). This includes mismatches in communication styles, time orientation, and gender roles (Hofstede, 2001; Hall, 1983). It is a necessity that policies must address cross-cultural collaboration through structured interaction. Community mediation programmes, such as the UK's 'Building Bridges' initiative, pair immigrant and host community members in joint projects to foster trust and shared norms (Cantle, 2012). Institutional reforms, e.g., flexible scheduling in public services and multilingual communication protocols, can further reduce coordination barriers.

Institutional incompatibility arises from divergent expectations about authority, law, and governance (see Chap. 5, Eq. 10). Immigrants from high power distance and collectivist societies may struggle with democratic participation, legal autonomy, and individual rights (Hofstede et al., 2010; House et al., 2004). Policies must therefore include institutional adaptation mechanisms. These might involve alternative dispute resolution systems that respect collective decision-making traditions, legal outreach programmes that explain rights and responsibilities in culturally resonant terms, and participatory governance models that include immigrant voices in local decision-making.

Each mechanism-specific intervention must be calibrated to the cultural distance profile of the target group. For example, immigrants from Confucian societies may benefit more from coordination-focused policies, while those from tribal or Islamic contexts may require institutional mediation. The CDIM provides the analytical tools to match mechanism to profile, enabling precision policy design.

Bidirectional Adaptation and Policy Symmetry

The CDIM's bidirectional adaptation model, formalized in Chap. 5 (Eqs. 11–13), challenges the traditional assumption that integration is a one-sided process in which immigrants adapt to a static host society. Instead, it posits that integration success depends on the simultaneous adaptation of both immigrant groups and host populations. This insight aligns with theoretical perspectives that emphasize mutual accommodation and the co-evolution of informal institutions (Kymlicka, 2010; Modood, 2013).

Informal institutions are not immutable. As Chap. 3 demonstrates, they evolve through interaction, negotiation, and collective endorsement (Searle, 2005; March & Olsen, 1989). However, such evolution requires deliberate policy support. Host societies must be prepared to adjust their normative expectations, institutional procedures, and social attitudes to accommodate cultural diversity. This does not imply normative relativism but rather a pragmatic recognition that rigid institutional frameworks can obstruct integration even when immigrants are willing to adapt (Rauhut, 2020).

Policy symmetry is therefore essential. Integration programmes must include components that target host society adaptation. These may involve diversity training for public sector employees, cultural competency development for educators and healthcare providers, and community engagement initiatives that foster intercultural dialogue.[1]

The CDIM's mathematical model reveals that mutual adaptation produces synergistic effects, enhancing integration outcomes beyond the additive contributions of each side (see Eq. 13). This suggests that investment in host society adaptation is not merely a moral imperative but a strategic necessity (see Rauhut & Laine, 2023; Borjas, 2019). Policies that neglect this dimension risk reinforcing normative asymmetries and perpetuating integration failure.

Contextual Adaptation and Dynamic Policy Calibration

Integration does not occur in a vacuum. The CDIM's dynamic threshold model (Eq. 14) demonstrates that the thresholds at which cultural distance becomes problematic are context-dependent. Economic opportunity, institutional flexibility, and political support can raise or lower these thresholds, altering the effectiveness of integration policies (Goodman, 2014; Joppke, 2007).

During periods of economic expansion, labour market openness and social optimism can mitigate the effects of cultural distance. Immigrants may find employment more easily, host populations may be more receptive, and institutions may have greater capacity for adaptation. In such contexts, even groups with moderate cultural divergence may integrate successfully with minimal intervention. Conversely, during economic downturns or political polarization, integration becomes more difficult even for culturally proximate groups (Bansak et al., 2021; Bodvardsson & Van den Berg, 2013). The same cultural distance that was manageable under favourable conditions may become overwhelming under stress.

Policies must therefore be dynamically calibrated. This requires monitoring systems that track economic indicators, political sentiment, and institutional capacity, and trigger appropriate adjustments in policy

[1] However, this recommendation presupposes that the host society consents to substantial immigration from a culturally distant population and, accordingly, accepts the need to adapt. In democratic systems, voters endorse the political positions they prefer, while politicians seeking (re)election must present policies that resonate with the electorate (Tullock, 1976). Consequently, if the electorate is unwilling to adapt, they will support political platforms asserting that no adjustment to the newcomers is required.

intensity (see Macuchova & Rauhut, 2023). For example, during economic recessions, governments may need to expand integration support for all groups, including those previously considered low risk. This could involve increasing funding for language programmes, expanding access to mental health services, and enhancing community mediation efforts.

Institutional flexibility is another critical variable. Rigid bureaucratic procedures, inflexible legal frameworks, and standardized service delivery models can exacerbate integration challenges (Gruber & Rauhut, 2023; Rauhut & Kettunen, 2024; Rauhut, 2026). Policies must therefore include institutional reform components that enhance responsiveness and adaptability.

Political support is equally important. Integration policies require sustained commitment from political leaders, public institutions, and civil society (Rauhut, 2026; Achard et al., 2025). In contexts where immigration is politicized or stigmatized, policy effectiveness may be undermined by lack of legitimacy or public resistance. If public opinion does not support the immigration policies of the incumbent government, that government in a democratic context must articulate the rationale for targeted integration policies, emphasize their empirical foundation, and underscore their benefits for social cohesion. Should these efforts prove unsuccessful, voters are likely to endorse alternative parties whose positions align more closely with their views.

Generational Policy Sequencing

Integration is a multi-generational process. The CDIM's generational model, discussed in Chap. 5, demonstrates that cultural distance diminishes over time but not uniformly. Each generation faces distinct challenges shaped by the interplay between inherited norms and host society expectations (Portes & Rumbaut, 2001; Alba & Nee, 2003).

First-generation immigrants often retain origin norms, particularly in domains such as family structure, gender roles, and religious practice. Policies targeting this group must focus on foundational support, including language acquisition, civic orientation, and basic institutional navigation. However, they must also recognize the limits of rapid adaptation. Forced assimilation can produce psychological stress, identity conflict, and social withdrawal (Berry, 2005; Gavrilets & Richerson, 2017). Instead, policies should facilitate gradual exposure to host society norms, provide mental health support, and create protected spaces for cultural negotiation.

Second-generation individuals face more complex challenges. They are socialized in the host society but often experience tension between family expectations and societal opportunities. This can produce acute identity conflicts, particularly around gender roles, career choices, and social behaviour (Achard et al., 2025; Schwartz et al., 2010). Policies must therefore include culturally sensitive education programmes and community support systems that facilitate intergenerational dialogue.

Third-generation integration typically involves convergence with host society norms but may still require support for heritage preservation and inclusive participation. Policies targeting this group should focus on ensuring that accumulated advantages translate into full social and economic inclusion (Zorlu & van Gent, 2023; Alba & Foner, 2015). This may involve affirmative action in education and employment, cultural heritage programmes, and civic engagement initiatives that promote pluralistic identity formation.

Generational sequencing is therefore essential. Policies must be designed with temporal depth, recognizing that integration unfolds over decades and that each generation requires a distinct set of interventions. The CDIM provides the analytical tools to model these trajectories, enabling policymakers to anticipate challenges and allocate resources accordingly.

Gender-Responsive Policy Framework

The CDIM's gender-differentiated integration model, discussed in Chap. 5, highlights the asymmetric impact of cultural distance on men and women. Gender norms, as a core component of informal institutions, interact with host society expectations in ways that produce systematically different integration trajectories (Kofman, 2004; Hofstede, 2001). This necessitates a gender-responsive policy framework that recognizes and addresses these differential experiences.

Women from societies with restrictive gender norms often face compounded barriers to integration. These include limited mobility, constrained educational and employment opportunities, and normative conflicts between family expectations and host society values (Inglehart & Norris, 2003; World Bank, 2012). Policies must therefore provide culturally sensitive support mechanisms. Examples include women-only integration programmes that respect gender segregation norms while facilitating exposure to host society institutions, childcare support that enables participation in language and employment schemes, and empowerment initiatives that provide resources for negotiating gender role transitions (Kofman et al., 2015; UNHCR, 2024).

Men from traditional societies may experience status anxiety and identity conflict when host society norms challenge established masculine roles. This can manifest in resistance to integration, withdrawal from institutional engagement, or reinforcement of patriarchal norms within immigrant communities (Goldin, 2021; Alesina et al., 2013). Policies must address these challenges through targeted programming that supports normative adaptation while preserving dignity. This may include male-focused mentorship schemes, intercultural dialogue on masculinity, and employment support that aligns with host society labour market expectations.

Gender integration patterns also evolve across generations. Second-generation women often experience acute tension between family cultural expectations and host society opportunities, requiring specialized support in education, career planning, and social participation (Alba & Foner, 2015). Third-generation gender patterns typically converge with host society norms but may benefit from heritage affirmation and inclusive institutional design (Zorlu & van Gent, 2023). Policies must therefore be sequenced and differentiated by gender and generation, recognizing the complex interplay between cultural distance and gendered socialization.

Spatially Adaptive Policy Architecture

Integration outcomes are shaped not only by cultural distance but also by spatial dynamics. As discussed in Chap. 3, informal institutions are geographically embedded, and their effects are amplified or mitigated by spatial arrangements (Penninx, 2003; Rauhut, 2020). The CDIM's spatial modelling reveals that identical integration strategies yield divergent outcomes across neighbourhoods, depending on enclave density, proximity to host institutions, and intercultural contact potential.

Spatial targeting implies differentiating policy interventions according to local cultural distance profiles. In high-density enclaves of culturally distant groups, standard policies such as language instruction and civic orientation must be augmented with community-based programmes that foster horizontal social connections (Bolt et al., 2010; Musterd & van Kempen, 2009; Brown et al., 2024).

Urban planning must be reconceptualized as integration policy. Housing allocation mechanisms should avoid reinforcing ethnic clustering and instead promote mixed residency patterns that enable bridging capital formation (Phillips et al., 2007). Policies that encourage voluntary dispersal through mobility support and incentives must balance against the risk of social fragmentation and displacement.

Resource Optimisation and Policy Efficiency

The CDIM's optimal policy mix framework, formalized in Chap. 5, provides mathematical tools for maximizing integration outcomes within budget constraints. This represents a significant advancement over traditional approaches that have relied on intuition and political preferences for resource allocation (Goodman, 2012; Joppke, 2007). The model demonstrates that optimal policy combinations vary systematically with cultural distance profiles, suggesting that resource allocation strategies must be tailored to specific immigrant group characteristics.

Policies exhibit complementary effects, where combinations of interventions produce greater impacts than the sum of individual programmes. For example, language training combined with employment support and cultural orientation produces synergistic effects that exceed the impact of each component alone (Berry, 1997). Integration policy must therefore be designed as coherent packages rather than collections of independent programmes.

Policy effectiveness also varies significantly with cultural distance. Groups experiencing overwhelming cultural differences may require fundamentally different approaches rather than simply more intensive versions of standard programmes (Berry, 1997; Ager & Strang, 2008; Colic-Peisker & Tilbury, 2007). For instance, refugees from tribal societies may benefit more from community-based mediation and long-term mentorship than from accelerated civic orientation courses.

Optimal policy combinations change over time as cultural distances shift, and contextual conditions evolve. This suggests that effective integration policy requires dynamic resource allocation systems that can redistribute investments based on changing needs and opportunities. Governments must develop monitoring systems that track integration outcomes, cultural distance indicators, and contextual variables, enabling evidence-based adjustments in policy design and resource distribution.

Implementation Challenges and Institutional Requirements

The transition from traditional uniform integration policies to precision approaches based on the CDIM framework requires significant institutional adaptations. The mathematical precision of the CDIM demands corresponding improvements in data collection, analysis capabilities, and programme delivery systems that may strain existing institutional capacities (Rauhut, 2026).

Effective implementation requires sophisticated assessment systems capable of measuring cultural distance profiles for different immigrant populations. This involves developing reliable instruments for measuring civilizational, dimensional, and developmental distance components, establishing data collection protocols, and creating analytical capabilities that translate measurements into policy recommendations. For example, the World Values Survey and Hofstede's cultural dimensions database provide foundational data but must be supplemented with localized assessments and longitudinal tracking.

Current immigration and integration institutions typically lack these capabilities, having been designed around uniform service delivery models. Developing CDIM implementation capacity requires substantial investments in staff training, technology systems, and analytical infrastructure. Resistance from established institutions and stakeholders may pose additional challenges, particularly where precision policies are perceived as complex or politically sensitive (Slootjes & Zanzuchi, 2023).

Precision integration policies also require coordination across multiple institutional levels and policy domains. Integration outcomes depend on interactions between local service delivery, regional economic conditions, national policy frameworks, and community-level dynamics (see Ferry, 2021).[2] Effective CDIM implementation requires institutional mechanisms

[2] Ferry (2021) does not discuss immigrant integration, but regional policy. He discusses the challenges of coordination across institutional levels and policy domains, highlighting how integration outcomes depend on the interplay between local service delivery, regional conditions, national frameworks, and community dynamics. Effective regional and integration policies require coordination across local, regional, and national levels, overcoming siloed approaches. In policy domains, the need to align different policy sectors (economic, social, administrative) to achieve coherent outcomes is highlighted. It also notes that outcomes are shaped by local service delivery capacity, regional economic disparities, and the coherence of national frameworks, which matches your phrasing. While framed in regional

that can coordinate these levels coherently, such as inter-ministerial task forces, regional integration councils, and community liaison offices.

Political Feasibility and Public Support

The CDIM framework's emphasis on differentiated policy approaches based on cultural distance profiles raises important questions about political feasibility and public support. While the mathematical framework provides scientific justification for differentiation, successful implementation requires navigating political dynamics that may resist explicit acknowledgement of cultural differences in policy design.

Traditional integration policy has often emphasized equality of treatment as a core principle, reflecting broader democratic commitments to equal treatment under law (Koopmans, 2010; Castles et al., 2014). The CDIM's emphasis on differentiated approaches may appear to conflict with these principles, requiring careful attention to political framing and public communication strategies. Policymakers must emphasize that precision policies are not discriminatory but evidence-based, designed to optimize integration outcomes for all groups.

The framework's emphasis on bidirectional adaptation provides important political advantages. By demonstrating that successful integration requires contributions from both immigrant populations and host societies, it reframes integration as a collective endeavour. This can help build broader coalitions for integration policy, including civil society organizations, local governments, and immigrant communities.

Public support can also be enhanced through transparency, accountability, and participatory governance. Integration policies must be explained clearly, evaluated rigorously, and adjusted responsively (IOM, 2022; Pasetti et al., 2024). Mechanisms such as citizen panels, immigrant advisory boards, and public reporting can foster trust and legitimacy, enabling precision policies to gain traction even in politically contested environments.

policy terms, the analysis recognizes that community engagement and local governance structures are critical for implementation success. These aspects are also highly relevant when it comes to immigrant integration.

When the Host Society Resists: Managing Native Non-acceptance

The CDIM framework presupposes bidirectional adaptation as a necessary condition for successful integration (see Chap. 5, Eq. 13). However, this assumption may not hold in contexts where the host population resists normative accommodation or rejects the legitimacy of immigrant presence altogether. As Chap. 3 outlines, informal institutions are sustained through collective recognition and endorsement (Searle, 2005; North, 1990). When native populations refuse to extend such recognition, integration becomes structurally impaired.

Research has shown that perceived cultural distance is a key driver of negative attitudes towards immigrants (Rauhut, 2020; Schwartz et al., 2010). Host society members may interpret divergent norms, particularly around gender roles, religious practice, and authority structures, as threats to social cohesion or national identity (Inglehart & Norris, 2003; Rothstein & Stolle, 2008). In such cases, integration policies must address not only immigrant adaptation but also native perception and normative anxiety.

Policy responses should begin with targeted public information campaigns that explain the rationale for integration, the benefits of diversity, and the mechanisms of cultural negotiation. These campaigns must be evidence-based, locally tailored, and emotionally resonant (Dodevska, 2024; Slootjes & Zanzuchi, 2022).

Second, governments must invest in intercultural contact infrastructure. Research consistently shows that structured, meaningful interaction between culturally distinct groups reduces prejudice and fosters mutual understanding (Cantle, 2012; Gelfand et al., 2024). Policies should therefore support joint community projects, intercultural schools, and inclusive public spaces that facilitate sustained engagement.

Third, institutional transparency and responsiveness are essential. Native populations must perceive integration policies as legitimate and accountable. This requires participatory governance mechanisms, such as citizen panels and local integration councils, that allow host society members to influence policy design and implementation. Such mechanisms can mitigate anti-elite sentiment and enhance democratic legitimacy (Goodman, 2014).

Finally, governments must be prepared to enforce anti-discrimination laws and protect immigrant rights. While persuasion and engagement are preferable, legal safeguards are necessary to ensure that native resistance does not translate into exclusionary practices or institutional bias (Farahat, 2021; European Commission, 2011). Integration cannot succeed in environments where immigrants are systematically denied access to housing, employment, or education due to informal prejudice.

When Immigrants Refuse to Adapt: Addressing Normative Intransigence

While much of the integration literature focuses on structural barriers and host society attitudes, the CDIM also recognizes that immigrant refusal to adapt can obstruct integration. Chapter 3 identifies informal institutions as deeply embedded systems of meaning-making that shape behaviour and identity (March & Olsen, 1989; Rauhut, 2020). In some cases, immigrants may actively resist host society norms, either due to ideological conviction, community pressure, or perceived moral superiority (Gavrilets & Richerson, 2017; Lazić & Pešić, 2024).

Such normative intransigence is particularly problematic when it involves rejection of core democratic principles, legal norms, or human rights standards. Examples include refusal to recognize gender equality, rejection of secular governance, or non-compliance with legal obligations. These behaviours not only hinder integration but may also provoke native backlash and undermine institutional trust (Koopmans, 2009; Joppke, 2007; Triandafyllidou, 2011; Modood, 2013).

Policy responses must be firm, principled, and proportionate. First, governments must clearly define non-negotiable normative baselines, e.g., respect for the rule of law, gender equality, and individual rights, and communicate these expectations during the early stages of integration. Civic orientation programmes must go beyond procedural instruction and engage immigrants in normative dialogue about the values underpinning host society institutions (OECD, 2024).

Second, conditionality mechanisms may be appropriate. Access to certain integration benefits, e.g., such as permanent residency, public housing, or employment subsidies, can be linked to demonstrable normative engagement. This does not imply coercion but rather a reciprocal model of integration in which rights are accompanied by responsibilities (Joppke, 2007; Kymlicka, 2010).

Third, governments should invest in community-level mediation and norm negotiation. Immigrant refusal to adapt is often reinforced by enclave dynamics, peer pressure, or misinformation (Cantle, 2012; Putnam, 2007; Council of Europe, 2008). Policies must therefore support local dialogue platforms, peer mentorship schemes, and culturally competent mediation services that facilitate internal normative evolution.

Fourth, enforcement mechanisms must be available when normative intransigence crosses into legal non-compliance. Governments must uphold the integrity of legal institutions and ensure that all residents, regardless of origin, are subject to the same rules and protections. This includes prosecuting, e.g., forced marriage, child marriage, honour-based violence, or educational neglect where they occur.

The Limits of Integration: When Public Support Erodes

The CDIM assumes that integration is possible when policies are well-designed, context-sensitive, and mutually adaptive. However, this assumption may not hold in contexts where public support for immigration, particularly from culturally distant societies, is absent or actively hostile. Chapter 3 warns that excessive cultural divergence can produce value dissonance and latent social fragmentation (Rauhut, 2020; Galtung, 1969). When governments pursue immigration policies that lack public legitimacy, they risk fuelling anti-immigration sentiment, populist backlash, and institutional erosion.

Policy realism is therefore essential. Governments must assess not only the technical feasibility of integration but also its political sustainability (Boswell, 2009; Geddes & Scholten, 2016). This requires robust public opinion monitoring, transparent policy communication, and strategic sequencing of immigration flows. For example, introducing culturally distant groups in small, well-supported cohorts may be more effective than large-scale resettlement without preparatory engagement.

Second, governments must avoid framing integration as a zero-sum game. Native populations often perceive immigration as a threat to economic opportunity, cultural identity, or institutional capacity (Esses et al., 2013; Putnam, 2007). Policies must therefore emphasize mutual benefit, shared responsibility, and inclusive development. This includes investing in public services, infrastructure, and social programmes that benefit both immigrants and natives (Ager & Strang, 2008; Scholten & van Breugel, 2018).

Third, elite consensus must be balanced with democratic responsiveness. While expert knowledge is essential for policy design, integration cannot succeed without public legitimacy. Governments must therefore engage citizens in deliberative processes, respond to local concerns, and adjust policies based on empirical feedback. Failure to do so risks reinforcing anti-elite narratives and undermining democratic trust (Rauhut, 2026).

Finally, governments must recognize that integration has limits. In some cases, cultural distance may be too great, institutional capacity too constrained, or public support too weak to sustain successful integration. In such contexts, alternative strategies, such as regional resettlement, temporary protection, or differentiated legal status, may be more appropriate. The CDIM provides the analytical tools to identify these thresholds and guide policy decisions accordingly.

Conclusion and Future Directions

The Cultural Distance Integration Model represents a fundamental advancement in integration policy theory and practice. By linking informal institutions to cultural distance and modelling their effects on integration outcomes, the CDIM provides a comprehensive framework for designing evidence-based interventions that are theoretically grounded, mathematically precise, and practically effective.

Precision integration policies, informed by the CDIM, move beyond uniform provision and embrace the complexity of cultural diversity. They recognize that integration is not a linear process but a dynamic negotiation between normative systems. By calibrating interventions to cultural distance profiles, addressing mechanism-specific barriers, supporting bidirectional adaptation, and optimizing resource allocation, these policies offer a roadmap for fostering inclusive, resilient societies.

Future research should focus on empirical validation of the CDIM's mathematical relationships, development of practical measurement instruments, and case study analyses of precision policy implementation. Policymakers must invest in institutional capacity, public communication, and participatory governance to realize the potential of precision integration. In doing so, they can move beyond the limitations of traditional approaches and build integration systems that are both just and effective.

References

Achard, P., Albrecht, S., Ghidoni, R., Cettolin, E., & Suetens, S. (2025). Local exposure to refugees changed attitudes to ethnic minorities in The Netherlands. *Economic Journal, 135*(667), 808–837. https://doi.org/10.1093/ej/ueae080

Ager, A., & Strang, A. (2008). Understanding integration: A conceptual framework. *Journal of Refugee Studies, 21*(2), 166–191. https://doi.org/10.1093/jrs/fen016

Alba, R., & Foner, N. (2015). *Strangers no more: Immigration and the challenges of integration in North America and Western Europe*. Princeton University Press.

Alba, R., & Nee, V. (2003). *Remaking the American mainstream: Assimilation and contemporary immigration*. Cambridge, Harvard University Press.

Alesina, A., Giuliano, P., & Nunn, N. (2013). On the origins of gender roles: Women and the plough. *Quarterly Journal of Economics, 128*(2), 469–530. https://doi.org/10.1093/qje/qjt005

Bansak, C., Simpson, N., & Zavodny, M. (2021). *The economics of immigration*. Routledge.

Berry, J. W. (1997). Immigration, acculturation, and adaptation. *Applied Psychology, 46*(1), 5–34. https://doi.org/10.1111/j.1464-0597.1997.tb01087.x

Berry, J. W. (2005). Acculturation: Living successfully in two cultures. *International Journal of Intercultural Relations, 29*(6), 697–712. https://doi.org/10.1016/j.ijintrel.2005.07.013

Bodvardsson, Ö. B., & Van den Berg, H. (2013). *The economics of immigration: Theory and policy*. Springer.

Bolt, G., Özuekren, A. S., & Phillips, D. (Eds.). (2010). *Linking integration and residential segregation*. Routledge.

Borjas, G. J. (2019). Reflections on immigration economics. In B. Elsner (Ed.), *Foundations of migration economics* (pp. 573–582). Oxford University Press.

Boswell, C. (2009). *The political uses of expert knowledge: Immigration policy and social research*. Cambridge University Press.

Brown, P., Gill, S., & Halsall, J. P. (2024). The impact of housing on refugees: An evidence synthesis. *Housing Studies, 39*(1), 227–271. https://doi.org/10.1080/02673037.2022.2045007

Cantle, T. (2012). *Interculturalism: The new era of cohesion and diversity*. Palgrave Macmillan.

Castles, S., de Haas, H., & Miller, M. J. (2014). *The age of migration: International population movements in the modern world*. Palgrave Macmillan.

Chemin, J. E., & Nagel, A. K. (2020). *Integration: Policies, practices and experiences.* German Country Report. Retrieved November 12, 2025, from https://respondmigration.com/wp-blog/refugee-integration-policies-practices-experiences-germany-country-report

Colic-Peisker, V., & Tilbury, F. (2007). *Refugees and employment: The effect of visible difference on discrimination.* Centre for Social and Community Research, Monash University. Retrieved November 11, 2025, from https://research-portal.murdoch.edu.au/esploro/outputs/report/Refugees-and-employment-The-effect-of/991005545406107891

Council of Europe. (2008). *White Paper on Intercultural Dialogue: Living Together as Equals in Dignity.* Launched by the Council of Europe Ministers of Foreign Affairs at their 118th Ministerial Session, Strasbourg, 7 May 2008.

Dodevska, I. (2024). The production of "evidence" for migrant integration policy in the European Union. *Migration Studies, 12*(4), mnae032. https://doi.org/10.1093/migration/mnae032

Esses, V. M., Medianu, S., & Lawson, A. S. (2013). Uncertainty, threat, and the role of the media in promoting the dehumanization of immigrants and refugees. *Journal of Social Issues, 69*(3), 518–536. https://doi.org/10.1111/josi.12027

European Commission. (2011). *European agenda for the integration of third-country nationals.* COM(2011) 455 final.

Farahat, A. (2021). Discrimination inside: Non-discrimination as a tool of migrant integration. *American Journal of International Law, 115*, 350–355. https://doi.org/10.1017/aju.2021.55

Ferry, M. (2021). Pulling things together: regional policy coordination approaches and drivers in Europe. *Policy and Society, 40*(1), 37–57. https://doi.org/10.1080/14494035.2021.1934985

Galtung, J. (1969). Violence, peace, and peace research. *Journal of Peace Research, 6*(3), 167–191. https://doi.org/10.1177/002234336900600301

Gavrilets, S., & Richerson, P. J. (2017). Collective action and the evolution of social norm internalization. *Proceedings of the National Academy of Sciences of the United States of America, 114*(23), 6068–6073. https://doi.org/10.1073/pnas.1703857114

Geddes, A., & Scholten, P. (2016). *The politics of migration and immigration in Europe* (2nd ed.).

Gelfand, M. J., Gavrilets, S., & Nunn, N. (2024). Norm dynamics: Interdisciplinary perspectives on social norm emergence, persistence, and change. *Annual Review of Psychology, 75*, 341–378. https://doi.org/10.1146/annurev-psych-033020-013319

Goldin, C. (2021). *Career and family: Women's century-long journey toward equity.* Princeton University Press.
Goodman, S. W. (2012). Fortifying citizenship: Policy strategies for civic integration in Western Europe. *World Politics, 64*(4), 659–698. https://doi.org/10.1017/S0043887112000190
Goodman, S. W. (2014). *Immigration and membership politics in Western Europe.* Cambridge University Press.
Gruber, M., & Rauhut, D. (2023). Immigrant integration in Austria and Sweden—A patchwork of multilevel governance and fragmented responsibilities. In J. Laine, D. Rauhut, & M. Gruber (Eds.), *Assessing the social impact of immigration in Europe: Renegotiating remoteness* (pp. 183–200). Edward Elgar.
Hall, E. T. (1983). *The dance of life: The other dimension of time.* Anchor Books.
Hofstede, G. (2001). *Culture's consequences: Comparing values, behaviours, institutions and organizations across nations* (2nd ed.). Sage Publications.
Hofstede, G., Hofstede, G. J., & Minkov, M. (2010). *Cultures and organizations: Software of the mind* (3rd ed.). McGraw-Hill.
House, R. J., Hanges, P. J., Javidan, M., Dorfman, P. W., & Gupta, V. (Eds.). (2004). *Culture, leadership, and organizations: The GLOBE study of 62 societies.* Sage Publications.
Inglehart, R., & Norris, P. (2003). *Rising tide: Gender equality and cultural change around the world.* Cambridge University Press.
IOM. (2022). *Toolkit for integrating migration into governance interventions.* Retrieved November 12, 2025, from https://migrationnetwork.un.org/resources/toolkit-integrating-migration-governance-interventions
Joppke, C. (2007). Beyond national models: Civic integration policies for immigrants in Western Europe. *West European Politics, 30*(1), 1–22. https://doi.org/10.1080/01402380601019613
Kofman, E. (2004). Family-related migration: A critical review of European studies. *Journal of Ethnic and Migration Studies, 30*(2), 243–262. https://doi.org/10.1080/1369183042000200687
Kofman, E., Saharso, S., & Vacchelli, E. (2015). Gendered perspectives on integration discourses and measures. *International Migration, 53*(4), 77–89. https://doi.org/10.1111/imig.12102
Koopmans, R. (2009). Trade-offs between equality and difference: Immigrant integration, multiculturalism and the welfare state in cross-National Perspective. *Journal of Ethnic and Migration Studies, 36*(1), 1–26. https://doi.org/10.1080/13691830903250881

Koopmans, R. (2010). Trade-Offs between equality and difference: immigrant Integration, multiculturalism and the welfare state in cross-national perspective. *Journal of Ethnic and Migration Studies, 36*(1), 1–26. https://doi.org/10.1080/13691830903250881

Kymlicka, W. (2010). The rise and fall of multiculturalism? New debates on inclusion and accommodation in diverse societies. *International Social Science Journal, 61*(199), 97–112. https://doi.org/10.1111/j.1468-2451.2010.01750.x

Lazić, M., & Pešić, J. (2024). Values, norms and social dynamics. *Philosophy and Society, 35*(3), 703–724. https://doi.org/10.2298/FID2403703L

Macuchova, Z., & Rauhut, D. (2023). Measuring immigrant integration—How, what and for whom? In D. Rauhut (Ed.), *New methods and theory on immigrant integration: Insights from remote and peripheral areas* (pp. 123–141). Edward Elgar.

March, J. G., & Olsen, J. P. (1989). *Rediscovering institutions: The organizational basis of politics.* Free Press.

Modood, T. (2013). *Multiculturalism: A civic idea* (2nd ed.). Polity Press.

Mügge, L., & van der Haar, M. (2016). Who is an immigrant and who requires integration? Categorizing in European policies. In B. Garcés-Mascareñas & R. Penninx (Eds.), *Integration processes and policies in Europe* (pp. 77–90). Springer.

Musterd, S., & van Kempen, R. (2009). Segregation and housing of minority ethnic groups in Western European cities. *Tijdschrift voor Economische en Sociale Geografie, 100*(4), 559–566. https://doi.org/10.1111/j.1467-9663.2009.00558.x

North, D. C. (1990). *Institutions, institutional change and economic performance.* Cambridge University Press.

OECD. (2024). *Settling in: Indicators of immigrant integration 2024.* OECD Publishing. https://doi.org/10.1787/9789264307216-en

Pasetti, F., Xhardez, C., Wisthaler, V., Conte, C., & Solano, G. (2024). An indicator-based approach to comparative policy analysis: Measuring regional governance of migrant integration. *Journal of Comparative Policy Analysis: Research and Practice, 26*(6), 648–668. https://doi.org/10.1080/13876988.2024.2375532

Penninx, R. (2003). Integration: The role of communities, institutions, and the state. *Migration Information Source.* https://www.migrationpolicy.org/article/integration-role-communities-institutions-and-state

Phillips, D., Davis, C., & Ratcliffe, P. (2007). Community cohesion and housing: A review of the evidence. *Joseph Rowntree Foundation.*

https://www.jrf.org.uk/report/community-cohesion-and-housing-review-evidence
Portes, A., & Rumbaut, R. G. (2001). *Legacies: The story of the immigrant second generation*. University of California Press.
Putnam, R. D. (2007). E pluribus Unum: Diversity and community in the twenty-first century. *Scandinavian Political Studies, 30*(2), 137–174. https://doi.org/10.1111/j.1467-9477.2007.00176.x
Rauhut, D. (2020). Integration and informal institutions. *Society, 57*(2), 211–218. https://doi.org/10.1007/s12115-020-00467-6
Rauhut, D. (2026). Rethinking immigrant integration theories for the 21st century. In B. Newbold & M. Crea-Arsenio (Eds.), *A research agenda for immigration settlement and adjustment* (pp. 9–29). Edward Elgar.
Rauhut, D., Aigner-Walder, M., & Schomaker, S. (2023). *Economics of immigration beyond the cities*. Palgrave Macmillan.
Rauhut, D., & Kettunen, P. (2024). Intergovernmental relations and refugee language training in Finland and Sweden: A conflicted policy process. In T. Bergström, S. Kuhlmann, M. Laffin, & E. Wayenberg (Eds.), *New perspectives on intergovernmental relations: Crisis and reform* (pp. 103–120). Palgrave Macmillan.
Rauhut, D., & Laine, J. (2023). Immigrant integration: A bordering perspective. In D. Rauhut (Ed.), *New methods and theory on immigrant integration: Insights from remote and peripheral areas* (pp. 68–85). Edward Elgar.
Rothstein, B., & Stolle, D. (2008). The state and social capital: An institutional theory of generalized trust. *Comparative Politics, 40*(4), 441–459. https://doi.org/10.5129/001041508X12911362383354
Scholten, P., & van Breugel, I. (Eds.). (2018). *Mainstreaming integration governance: New trends in migrant integration policies in Europe*. Palgrave Macmillan.
Schwartz, S. J., Unger, J. B., Zamboanga, B. L., & Szapocznik, J. (2010). Rethinking the concept of acculturation: Implications for theory and research. *American Psychologist, 65*(4), 237–251. https://doi.org/10.1037/a0019330
Searle, J. R. (2005). What is an institution? *Journal of Institutional Economics, 1*(1), 1–22. https://doi.org/10.1017/S1744137405000020
Slootjes, J., & Zanzuchi, M. B. (2023). *Toolkit for evidence-informed policymaking in migrant integration*. Migration Policy Institute Europe.
Triandafyllidou, A. (2011). *Immigrants and National Identity in Europe*. Routledge.
Tullock, G. (1976). *The vote motive*. The Institute of Economic Affairs.
UNHCR. (2024). *Integration handbook: Gender section*. Retrieved November 11, 2025, from https://www.unhcr.org/handbooks/ih/age-gender-diversity/gender

World Bank. (2012). World development report 2012: Gender equality and development. *World Bank Publications*. https://doi.org/10.1596/978-0-8213-8810-5

Zorlu, A., & van Gent, W. (2023). Economic assimilation of the "third generation": An intergenerational mobility perspective. *International Migration Review, 58*(2), 734–763. https://doi.org/10.1177/01979183231165499

CHAPTER 7

Reframing the Debate

This discussion chapter serves to connect the threads developed throughout the book. Earlier chapters established the conceptual foundations of cultural distance, examined its institutional and theoretical dimensions, and formalized the Cultural Distance Integration Model mathematically. This chapter now situates CDIM within the broader landscape of integration theories, bridging institutional economics with assimilationist, multiculturalist, critical, and constructivist traditions. By doing so, it highlights both complementarities and tensions, showing where CDIM aligns with existing insights and where it departs to offer new explanatory power. This integrative perspective reframes the debate, positioning cultural distance not as a peripheral concept but as a central determinant of integration outcomes and policy design.

Institutional Economics and Immigrant Integration

A central contribution of this study lies in its explicit anchoring within the tradition of institutional economics. By foregrounding culture as an informal institution, the Cultural Distance Integration Model (CDIM) extends the analytical reach of institutional theory into the domain of migration and integration. North's (1990) seminal definition of institutions as 'humanly devised constraints that structure political, economic and social interaction' provides the foundation for this approach. Integration

D. Rauhut, *Institutional Economics and Immigrant Integration*,
https://doi.org/10.1007/978-3-032-28361-0_7

outcomes are not reducible to individual choices or structural opportunities alone; they are mediated by the interplay of formal and informal institutions that confer legitimacy, coordinate behaviour, and stabilize expectations. In this respect, CDIM demonstrates that cultural distance functions as a constraint analogous to transaction costs in markets, shaping the feasibility and efficiency of social coordination. The model thereby situates integration within the broader logic of institutional economics, where adaptation and legitimacy are prerequisites for sustainable interaction (Greif, 2006; Williamson, 2000; Ostrom, 2005).

This institutional framing also highlights the dynamic nature of integration. Institutions are not static; they evolve through feedback, negotiation, and contestation. As Aoki (2001) has argued, institutional change often emerges from the interaction between formal rules and informal norms, producing hybrid arrangements that reflect both continuity and adaptation. CDIM captures this dynamic by modelling integration as institutional alignment rather than mere social convergence. It shows that integration succeeds when cultural distance remains within manageable bounds, but falters when divergence exceeds thresholds that undermine legitimacy and coordination. In this way, CDIM contributes to a more rigorous understanding of how informal institutions condition the success or failure of policy interventions, while also affirming the bidirectional nature of adaptation between immigrants and host societies.

The broader literature on institutional economics demonstrates that successful institutional change has historically fostered growth, prosperity, and social stability. Acemoglu and Robinson (2012) argue that inclusive institutions, which secure property rights, encourage innovation, enable broad participation, and underpin long-term economic development. Conversely, extractive or rigid institutions have often produced stagnation, inequality, and political instability. The trajectory of institutional change thus determines whether societies harness diversity as a source of dynamism or succumb to fragmentation and inefficiency. CDIM situates immigrant integration within this logic: when institutional adaptation succeeds, integration can contribute to prosperity and cohesion; when it fails, the result may be exclusion, mistrust, and diminished collective welfare.

Failure to achieve institutional alignment in the context of migration carries significant economic, social, and institutional consequences. If immigrant integration receives little support among natives, due to non-adjustment of informal institutions, the legitimacy of integration policies may be undermined, producing resistance and political backlash. Similarly, if immigrants refuse to adjust their informal institutions, the result may be parallel societies, weakened social trust, and coordination failures in labour markets, education, and civic participation. Such outcomes resonate with Putnam's (2007) findings on diversity and social capital, where lack of bridging institutions can erode trust and cooperation. In institutional economic terms, persistent cultural distance without adaptation increases transaction costs, reduces efficiency, and destabilizes the legitimacy of both formal and informal rules. CDIM highlights that integration is not merely a technical process but a systemic negotiation, where failure to adjust on either side risks undermining the foundations of prosperity and cohesion.

Epistemological Perspectives

The epistemological consequences of this approach are profound. Hitherto, immigrant integration research has been dominated by interpretivist methodologies, Marxist critiques, qualitative case studies, and ethnographic analyses (Anthias, 2013; Castles, 2010; Favell, 2003). These traditions have provided invaluable insights into lived experience, power asymmetries, and the social construction of identity, but they have often remained descriptive, context-specific, and resistant to generalization. CDIM represents a fundamentally different epistemological orientation. By embedding integration analysis within institutional economics and employing mathematical formalization, it shifts the field towards prediction, optimization, and comparative generalizability. This does not displace qualitative or critical approaches but complements them by offering a systematic framework capable of identifying structural constraints and threshold dynamics that qualitative research can then explore in depth. In this sense, CDIM exemplifies what Abbott (2004) has termed 'analytic sociology', where formal models provide the *framework* for understanding complex social processes.

Moreover, CDIM challenges the epistemological monopoly of interpretivist paradigms by demonstrating that integration can be studied not only as narrative and discourse but also as a system of institutional compatibility subject to measurable constraints. This shift resonates with the broader movement in the social sciences towards methodological pluralism (Rauhut, 2023; Hedström & Bearman, 2009). It acknowledges the value of ethnographic and critical perspectives while insisting that predictive modelling can enrich the field by identifying patterns, thresholds, and causal mechanisms that are otherwise obscured. Epistemologically, CDIM thus redefines integration research as a domain where formal and interpretive approaches must co-exist, each illuminating different dimensions of the phenomenon.

Finally, the adoption of Becker-inspired modelling within institutional economics situates integration research within a tradition of social science that seeks to extend economic reasoning to domains traditionally considered beyond its reach. Just as Becker demonstrated that family behaviour, crime, and education could be analysed through economic models, CDIM shows that cultural distance and integration dynamics can be formalized without losing sight of their normative and political dimensions. This epistemological move expands the boundaries of institutional economics, positioning it as a discipline capable of addressing one of the most pressing challenges of contemporary societies: how to manage diversity in ways that foster legitimacy, prosperity, and cohesion. In doing so, CDIM not only advances integration research but also contributes to the evolution of institutional economics itself, demonstrating its relevance to domains of social life that have hitherto been analysed primarily through interpretivist or critical lenses.

An Omitted Variable Problem?

The absence of informal institutions and culture in much of the integration literature can indeed be conceptualized as a form of omitted variable bias. Mainstream analyses have traditionally emphasized structural indicators such as employment, education, housing, and language acquisition. These are measurable, comparable across contexts, and relatively straightforward to operationalize. Yet by excluding informal institutions, i.e., norms, values, trust, legitimacy, and cultural repertoires, such studies risk mis-specifying the causal model. In econometric terms, if culture systematically influences integration outcomes but is not included in the model, the estimated effects of the included variables may be biased or misleading (Wooldridge, 2010). For example, labour market participation might appear to be explained by education alone, when in reality cultural distance and normative expectations about gender roles or authority also play a decisive role. This omission distorts both the explanatory power of models and the policy prescriptions derived from them. It leaves both the *explanans* and the *explanandum* with a significant *lacuna*, insofar as the causal mechanisms and the outcomes they are meant to explain remain only partially specified.

Institutional economics has long emphasized that both formal and informal institutions jointly shape economic and social outcomes. North (1990) argued that informal institutions are often more resilient than formal rules, precisely because they are embedded in social norms and collective expectations. Greif (2006) demonstrated how informal institutions such as reputation and trust sustained medieval trade networks, while Acemoglu and Robinson (2012) showed that inclusive institutions underpin long-term prosperity. Ignoring informal institutions in integration research is therefore equivalent to omitting a key explanatory variable. The consequence is that models may overstate the efficacy of time, exposure, or structural interventions, while underestimating the friction generated by cultural distance. This helps explain why some integration trajectories remain stubbornly resistant to policy interventions despite favourable structural conditions.

The methodological implications are significant. Omitted variable bias not only weakens the explanatory capacity of integration research but also undermines its predictive validity. As Heckman (2000) has argued in the context of labour economics, models that fail to account for unobserved heterogeneity risk producing misleading estimates of policy effectiveness. In integration studies, the non-use of informal institutions has produced a similar blind spot: policies designed around structural indicators alone often fail to deliver expected outcomes because they ignore the cultural and normative constraints that shape behaviour. CDIM corrects for this by explicitly incorporating culture as a measurable variable, thereby improving model specification and reducing bias. In doing so, it aligns integration research with the methodological standards of institutional economics, where both formal and informal institutions are treated as co-determinants of social order.

The policy implications of this omission are considerable. When informal institutions are ignored, policymakers risk designing interventions that are misaligned with the lived realities of immigrant populations and host societies. Language instruction, employment support, and housing provision may be necessary but insufficient if cultural distance remains unaddressed. Moreover, neglecting informal institutions can exacerbate mistrust among natives, who may perceive integration policies as ineffective or illegitimate. Similarly, immigrants may experience frustration if their cultural repertoires are pathologized or ignored. By treating culture as an omitted variable, integration research has inadvertently contributed to policy failures and political backlash. CDIM offers a corrective by operationalizing cultural distance, enabling policymakers to design interventions that are both empirically grounded and institutionally sensitive. In this way, the model not only advances academic rigour but also enhances the legitimacy and effectiveness of integration policy.

Finally, the theoretical consequences are equally profound. By neglecting informal institutions, much of the integration literature has implicitly assumed that culture is either irrelevant or destined to converge automatically over time. This assumption mirrors assimilationist theories that posit integration as a linear process of gradual convergence (Gordon, 1964; Alba & Nee, 2003). Yet empirical evidence shows that cultural distance can persist across generations, producing enduring frictions in labour markets, education, and civic participation (Portes & Rumbaut, 2001). Treating culture as an omitted variable obscures these dynamics and reinforces overly optimistic narratives about the inevitability of integration. CDIM challenges this by demonstrating that cultural distance is not a residual factor but a central determinant of institutional compatibility, one that must be explicitly modelled if integration research is to capture the complexity of real-world outcomes.

Situating CDIM Among Competing Paradigms

The field of immigrant integration has been characterized by theoretical diversity, with different schools of thought offering competing explanations for integration outcomes. From the early Chicago School's straight-line assimilation theory to contemporary critical approaches questioning the very foundations of integration discourse, scholars have grappled with fundamental questions about how cultural differences affect social incorporation, what constitutes successful integration, and whose responsibility it is to facilitate this process.

Assimilation Theories and CDIM

The Chicago School's classical assimilation theory, developed by Park and Burgess in the 1920s, conceptualized integration as a linear, unidirectional process whereby immigrants gradually shed their original cultural characteristics and adopt those of the host society (Park & Burgess, 1921; Gordon, 1964). This 'straight-line' model assumed that cultural distance would naturally diminish over time and generations, leading to eventual complete assimilation.

CDIM both builds upon and challenges this classical framework. The model's generational dynamics component (Eq. 16: $CD_{gen}(n) = CD_{initial} \times \rho n + (1\text{-}\rho n) \times CD_{equilibrium}$) acknowledges the temporal dimension emphasized by Chicago School theorists. However, CDIM introduces several critical modifications. The first deals with *nonlinear dynamics*. Unlike the linear progression assumed by classical theory, CDIM's threshold model (Eq. 3) demonstrates that integration success can experience dramatic shifts at critical cultural distance points. This suggests that the Chicago School's assumption of gradual, steady progress may be overly simplistic. The second modification relates to a *persistent cultural distance*. The model's inclusion of $CD_{equilibrium}$ recognizes that some cultural differences may persist permanently, challenging the classical assumption of complete assimilation. This aligns with contemporary critiques of the 'melting pot' metaphor (Alba & Nee, 2003). Lastly, there is a need for a *bidirectional adaptation*. CDIM's bidirectional adaptation model (Eqs. 11–13) explicitly contradicts the one-way adaptation assumed by classical theory, incorporating host society changes alongside immigrant adaptation.

The new assimilation theory, developed by Alba and Nee (2003), refined classical approaches by acknowledging that assimilation could take multiple forms and that host societies also change in response to immigration. This 'bumpy-line' assimilation recognized setbacks and variations in integration trajectories while maintaining that general convergence towards mainstream society remained the dominant pattern.

CDIM aligns closely with new assimilation theory's key insights while providing mathematical precision to previously qualitative observations. First, it acknowledges *multidimensional integration*. Both approaches recognize that integration occurs across multiple domains (economic, social, cultural, political). CDIM's domain-specific threshold model (Eq. 15) formalizes this insight, allowing for systematic analysis of how cultural distance affects different life domains differently. Second, there is a need to allow *contextual variation*. New assimilation theory emphasizes that integration outcomes depend heavily on context. CDIM's dynamic threshold model (Eq. 14) mathematically captures this insight, showing how economic opportunities, institutional flexibility, and political support alter the relationship between cultural distance and integration success. Third, *bidirectional change* is a central component. Both frameworks acknowledge that integration involves mutual adaptation. CDIM provides mathematical tools for modelling this bidirectional process, quantifying how both immigrant and host society characteristics change over time.

Segmented assimilation theory, developed by Portes and Zhou (1993) and Portes and Rumbaut (2001), challenged the assumption that all immigrant groups follow similar integration trajectories. Instead, it proposed three possible paths: upward assimilation into the middle class, downward assimilation into the urban underclass, and selective acculturation maintaining ethnic identity while achieving economic success.

CDIM's threshold dynamics provide a mathematical framework for understanding the mechanisms underlying segmented assimilation. First, *threshold effects* must be acknowledged. The model's identification of critical cultural distance thresholds (T1 and T2) offers a potential explanation for why some groups experience upward mobility while others face downward assimilation. Groups with cultural distances below T1 may follow the upward path, while those above T2 may face systemic barriers. Second, a *contextual sensitivity* is needed. CDIM's dynamic threshold model shows how the same cultural distance can lead to different outcomes depending on structural conditions. This formalizes segmented assimilation's insight that context matters more than individual characteristics. Third, *policy implications* are important. The model's policy intervention framework (Eqs. 22–24) provides tools for understanding how targeted interventions might help groups avoid downward assimilation trajectories.

Hartmut Esser's multidimensional integration theory conceptualizes integration as occurring across four dimensions: cultural (language, values), structural (education, employment), social (friendships, networks), and identificational (belonging, citizenship) (Esser, 2001). This framework has been particularly influential in European integration research.

CDIM complements Esser's multidimensional approach while adding mathematical precision. (1) *Domain specificity*: CDIM's domain-specific threshold model (Eq. 15) provides mathematical tools for analysing integration across different life domains, similar to Esser's dimensions. (2) *Interdependence*: both frameworks recognize that integration dimensions are interconnected. CDIM's composite cultural distance function (Eq. 2) captures these interactions through its interaction terms. (3) *Dynamic processes*: while Esser's theory describes integration dimensions, CDIM provides mathematical models for understanding how these processes unfold over time and how they can be influenced by policy interventions.

Co-existence Theories and CDIM

Multicultural theory, developed by scholars like Kymlicka (1996) and Modood (2007), challenges assimilationist assumptions by arguing that cultural diversity is valuable and that integration should not require cultural homogenization. Instead, successful integration involves maintaining cultural distinctiveness while participating fully in broader society.

CDIM engages with multicultural theory in several important ways: first, it addresses *persistent cultural differences*. The model's recognition that $CD_{equilibrium}$ may remain above zero aligns with multicultural expectations that some cultural differences will and should persist. This represents a significant departure from classical assimilation assumptions. Second, it acknowledges *institutional adaptation*. CDIM's host society adaptation function (Eq. 12) formalizes multicultural theory's emphasis on institutional accommodation. The model shows how institutional flexibility (IF) affects integration outcomes. Third, it develops the *policy framework*. The model's policy intervention framework can be interpreted as supporting multicultural approaches by identifying how policies can facilitate integration without requiring cultural assimilation.

However, CDIM also presents challenges to multicultural theory. First, the *threshold limits* challenge the multicultural theory. The model suggests that there are limits to how much cultural distance can be accommodated before integration becomes difficult. This implies that unlimited cultural diversity may not be sustainable. Second, the (theoretical) *quantification of differences* between multiculturalism and the CDIM places them in diametral positions. By mathematically modelling cultural distance, CDIM may inadvertently essentialize cultural differences in ways that multicultural theorists would critique.

The concept of superdiversity, introduced by Vertovec (2007), emphasizes the complex, multiple, and intersecting dimensions of contemporary migration. This approach argues that traditional categories of ethnicity and nationality are inadequate for understanding contemporary migration patterns.

CDIM's multidimensional approach to cultural distance aligns with superdiversity's emphasis on complexity: first, both present a *multidimensional framework*. The model's three-level cultural distance calculation (civilizational, dimensional, developmental) captures some of the complexity emphasized by superdiversity theorists. Second, both press on *intersectionality*. CDIM's gender-differentiated model (Eqs. 18–21) recognizes that cultural distance affects different groups differently, acknowledging intersectional effects. Third, both allow for a *contextual variation*. The model's dynamic thresholds capture how the same cultural characteristics can have different implications in different contexts.

Interculturalism, developed by theorists like Cantle (2012), Zapata-Barrero (2016), and Zapata-Barrero and Mansouri (2022), emphasizes dialogue, interaction, and mutual adaptation between cultural groups. This approach sees integration as an ongoing process of negotiation and exchange rather than a one-way adaptation (Meer & Modood, 2012).

CDIM's bidirectional adaptation model directly formalizes interculturalist insights: first, *mutual adaptation* is a starting point. The model's separate functions for immigrant adaptation (Eq. 11) and host society adaptation (Eq. 12) mathematically capture the bilateral nature of integration emphasized by interculturalism. Second, there are *synergistic effects* in integration processes. The combined integration success function (Eq. 13) includes an interaction term that captures how mutual adaptation can create synergistic effects beyond the sum of individual adaptations. Third, both advocate *dynamic processes*. Both frameworks emphasize that integration is an ongoing process rather than a fixed outcome.

Critical Traditions and CDIM

The fundamental distinction between the Cultural Distance Integration Model (CDIM) and the three critical theoretical frameworks lies in their conceptualization of adaptation processes and power relations within integration contexts. While CDIM operates from a bidirectional framework that envisions mutual accommodation between immigrant communities and receiving societies, Critical Race Theory, Post-Colonial Theory, and Whiteness Studies approach integration through a more asymmetrical lens that emphasizes structural inequalities and historical power imbalances.

CDIM's theoretical foundation assumes that successful integration emerges through reciprocal adjustments, where both newcomers and established populations modify certain practices and expectations to achieve greater social cohesion. This bidirectional approach treats cultural adaptation as a negotiated process involving compromises from multiple parties. In contrast, the three critical frameworks tend to interpret any expectation of immigrant adaptation as potentially problematic, viewing such requirements through the lens of historical and contemporary power structures. From these perspectives, requests for immigrant adjustment, regardless of corresponding expectations for majority population accommodation, risk reproducing colonial patterns of cultural dominance and may inadvertently perpetuate systemic inequalities that privilege dominant group norms while marginalizing minority cultural expressions and ways of being.

Critical Race Theory (CRT), developed by legal scholars like Bell (1987) and Crenshaw (1991), emphasizes how race and racism structure social relations and institutional practices. CRT scholars have increasingly brought their analytical lens to migration studies, highlighting how white employers commend Latinos for what they view as submissive behaviour, while simultaneously upholding existing racial hierarchies (Golash-Boza, 2010).

CDIM's relationship with CRT reveals both potential synergies and significant tensions: first, the role of *structural analysis*. CRT's emphasis on structural racism could enhance CDIM by incorporating how racialization affects the threshold points and policy effectiveness measures in the model. Second, the role of *power dynamics*. CRT's focus on power relations challenges CDIM's potentially neutral treatment of cultural distance. The model's institutional incompatibility measure (Eq. 10) could be reconceptualized to explicitly account for how dominant group power shapes which differences are seen as problematic. Third, the role of *whiteness as a norm*. CRT scholars have critiqued the 'whiteness' of integration research, arguing that integration models implicitly assume white, Western norms as the standard against which others are measured. CDIM's mathematical framework could inadvertently reinforce these assumptions unless explicitly addressed. Fourth, this relates to a *methodological critique*. CRT scholars might argue that mathematical modelling, by appearing objective and neutral, obscures the subjective and political nature of integration processes.

Post-colonial theory, developed by scholars like Said (1978), Spivak (1988), and Bhabha (1994), examines how colonial power relations continue to shape contemporary social relations. Applied to migration studies, post-colonial theory critiques integration discourse as potentially reproducing colonial power structures.

CDIM and post-colonial theory may disagree in several important ways. Firstly, *knowledge production*. Post-colonial scholars have called for an end to neocolonial knowledge production in integration research, arguing that current approaches reproduce colonial epistemologies. CDIM's mathematical framework could be seen as continuing Western, scientific approaches to understanding non-Western populations. Secondly, *cultural hierarchies.* Post-colonial theory critiques how cultural differences are often interpreted through hierarchical frameworks that privilege Western cultural forms. CDIM's civilizational distance component (Eq. 5) could inadvertently reproduce these hierarchies unless carefully constructed. Thirdly, *agency and resistance.* Post-colonial theory emphasizes how colonized peoples resist and subvert dominant narratives. CDIM's current formulation may not adequately capture immigrant agency and resistance to integration pressures.

Whiteness studies, developed by scholars like Frankenberg (1993) and Roediger (1991), examines how whiteness functions as a racial category and system of privilege. This field understands whiteness as a dominant force shaping cultural, social, political, and economic systems, influencing both daily life and institutional structures throughout Western societies (Efird et al., 2024; Olcoń, 2023).

CDIM's relationship with whiteness studies highlights several critical considerations. The first consideration relates to *normative assumptions.* Whiteness studies would critique CDIM's potential assumption that integration success means approximating white, Western norms. The model's cultural distance measures could be reconceptualized to avoid reproducing white supremacist assumptions. Moreover, a white Westerner living in a culturally distant country would experience the same challenges as culturally distant immigrants do in white Western countries today. The second consideration relates to *invisible privileges.* The model's context-dependent thresholds might reflect how whiteness operates as an invisible privilege that makes integration easier for some groups than others. The third consideration relates to *methodological whiteness.* The emphasis on mathematical modelling itself might be seen as reflecting white, Western epistemological preferences that marginalize other ways of knowing.

Constructivist Approaches and CDIM

Constructivist approaches, influenced by scholars like Berger and Luckmann (1966) and Geertz (1973), emphasize that culture is not a fixed essence but rather is continuously constructed and reconstructed through social interaction. This perspective challenges essentialist understandings of cultural difference.

CDIM's treatment of culture raises important constructivist concerns. The first relates to *cultural essentialism*. The model's quantification of cultural distance could be interpreted as treating culture as a fixed, measurable entity rather than a dynamic, constructed phenomenon. The second concern relates to *dynamic construction*. However, CDIM's generational model (Eq. 16) does acknowledge that cultural characteristics change over time, aligning with constructivist insights about cultural fluidity. The third relates to *contextual meaning*. The model's recognition that the same cultural distance can have different effects in different contexts reflects constructivist insights about the contextual nature of cultural meaning.

Boundary-making theory, developed by scholars like Barth (1969) and Wimmer (2013), emphasizes how social boundaries are actively constructed, maintained, and transformed through social processes. This approach focuses on how boundaries between groups are created and policed rather than taking group differences as given.

CDIM could eventually benefit from incorporating boundary-making insights. *Boundary permeability*: the model's threshold dynamics could be reconceptualized as reflecting the permeability of social boundaries rather than fixed cultural distances. *Boundary maintenance*: the model's policy intervention framework could incorporate how policies affect boundary-making processes, not just individual adaptation. *Dynamic boundaries*: the recognition that boundaries can shift over time could enhance CDIM's understanding of how integration processes unfold.

Synthesis and Implications

Theoretical Contributions of CDIM

CDIM makes several important contributions to the theoretical landscape of integration research. The first contribution is about *mathematical precision*. Unlike most existing theories, CDIM provides mathematical tools for generating precise predictions about integration outcomes. This moves the field beyond descriptive analysis towards predictive modelling. A second contribution relates to the *threshold identification*. The model's recognition of nonlinear relationships and tipping points adds important nuance to integration theory. This insight helps explain why some integration processes succeed while others fail, even under apparently similar conditions. The model also contributes by its *policy optimization*. CDIM's policy intervention framework provides concrete tools for policy optimization that most existing theories cannot offer. This bridges the gap between theoretical insights and practical applications. A fourth contribution is its inclusion of *multidimensional complexity*. The model's multidimensional approach to cultural distance captures complexity that simpler theoretical frameworks miss. Another contribution is its *bidirectional dynamics*. CDIM's formal modelling of bidirectional adaptation provides mathematical precision to insights that have remained largely qualitative in other theoretical approaches.

Theoretical Criticism

Despite its contributions, CDIM will inevitably attract theoretically based criticism from diverse academic traditions. These critiques are not only expected; they are vital to the model's development and its dialogue with broader scholarship. In what follows, five central areas of potential criticism are briefly discussed and addressed, including reductionism, power dynamics, cultural essentialism, normative assumptions, and methodological nationalism. Each response acknowledges the concern while demonstrating how CDIM either accommodates, challenges, or is compatible with alternative perspectives. One such criticism relates to *reductionism concerns*. Critics, particularly from critical traditions, will argue that mathematical modelling oversimplifies complex social processes and reduces rich cultural phenomena to numerical relationships. While CDIM necessarily abstracts aspects of social complexity, this abstraction is not simplification for its own sake. Instead, it is a deliberate methodological strategy to reveal patterns that would otherwise remain obscured in purely qualitative accounts. Mathematical modelling in CDIM complements, but *not replaces*, critical reflection by offering a structured lens through which nuance can be analysed, tested, and debated.

A second criticism relates to *power dynamics*. The model will receive criticism because it does allegedly not adequately account for how power relations and structural inequalities shape integration processes. CDIM does not claim to fully encapsulate all dimensions of power and inequality. However, it does offer a framework through which their influence can be inferred and examined across contexts. Rather than ignoring power relations, the model's structure enables these forces to emerge through variable interactions and comparative outcomes. It invites further exploration, not exclusion, of structural influences that shape integration processes.

A third criticism relates to *cultural essentialism*. The quantification of cultural distance will be accused of treating culture as fixed and measurable rather than dynamic and constructed. CDIM acknowledges that culture is not static; it is fluid, contested, and continuously reshaped through interaction. The model's quantification of cultural distance is not a claim to objectivity, but a heuristic tool that helps structure comparative inquiry. Rather than essentializing, CDIM operationalizes cultural factors in ways that remain open to reinterpretation, contextual variation, and dialogue with qualitative insights. The formulation of the model makes it flexible and interpretive, not dogmatic or reductive.

A fourth criticism will be accusations of *normative assumptions*. The model will be accused of implicitly assuming that integration success means approximating dominant group norms, potentially reproducing existing power structures. However, CDIM explicitly avoids normative hierarchies by categorizing cultures on a nominal scale, i.e., there is no implicit ranking, no dominant norm. The model's premise of bilateral adjustment rejects the idea that integration equates to conformity with majority standards. Instead, CDIM emphasizes mutual transformation across cultural boundaries, reinforcing integration as a dynamic process rather than a one-sided assimilation.

A last criticism will be based on accusations of *methodological nationalism*. The focus on national-level cultural differences may miss subnational variations and transnational connections that are increasingly important in contemporary migration. CDIM uses national-level cultural indicators as a foundational scaffold, not as a boundary. The model explicitly analyses spatial differences and the contextual dynamics in which they unfold, allowing for the detection of patterns across subnational regions and transnational connections. Rather than assuming cultural homogeneity within national borders, CDIM accommodates complexity by embedding integration processes within their geographic and social environments.

Nonetheless, social science is neither objective nor value-free (Rauhut, 2023). Potential criticisms of the CDIM warrant careful reflection. It is important to recognize, however, that such critiques often stem from fundamentally different epistemological standpoints. The areas in which tensions (or at the very least, dissonance) arise between CDIM and theories belonging to the critical paradigm (critical race theory, post-colonialism, and whiteness studies), and to some extent with constructivist perspectives, can be traced back to fundamental epistemological differences. CDIM is grounded in principles such as mathematical logic, quantifiability, generalizability, and objective data. These stand in stark contrast to the foundations of the critical paradigm and constructivist theories, which draw upon phenomenology, hermeneutics, postmodernism, subjective data, and an understanding of the researcher as an engaged activist (Rauhut, 2023). Given such profoundly divergent epistemological premises, it is far from surprising that different aspects of the same phenomena are examined, often leading to contrasting conclusions (Bryman, 2006).

While CDIM, alongside theories within the co-existence paradigm and assimilation theories, assumes that cultural adaptation occurs over time, theories representing the critical paradigm interpret such adaptation as a central mechanism of oppression. Without reciprocal adaptation by both immigrants to the host society and the host society to the immigrants, no genuine integration can occur. However, from the critical paradigm perspective, such adaptation perpetuates the oppression of the host society. In light of these fundamentally opposing premises, the significant tensions between CDIM and the critical paradigm perspective are readily understandable.

Conclusion

The Cultural Distance Integration Model (CDIM) marks a significant leap forward in the study of integration processes, offering a mathematically rigorous framework for simulating and understanding the nuanced dynamics between immigrant and native populations. Building upon and departing from existing paradigms, CDIM enables researchers to generate precise, testable predictions about integration trajectories, while also retaining the complexity and multidimensionality that characterize real-world social interactions.

At the heart of CDIM lies its ability to operationalize threshold dynamics and bidirectional adaptation mechanisms, i.e., two features that allow the model to reflect not only how individuals respond to social distance but also how policy interventions and environmental changes may influence collective outcomes over time. This approach has proven valuable in optimizing policy decisions, offering practical tools to balance cultural diversity with the goals of social cohesion and economic inclusion. Unlike traditional models that often rely on static assumptions or unidirectional assimilation narratives, CDIM enables feedback loops, tipping points, and contextual sensitivity, i.e., all of which are essential for capturing the lived realities of integration.

To situate CDIM within the broader theoretical landscape, the conceptual illustration in Fig. 7.1 maps five paradigms that define common views on the immigrant-native relationship: *assimilation*, *co-existence*, *critical*, *constructivist*, and the *CDIM* focused on mutual adaptation. Each paradigm represents a distinct orientation, ranging from the expectation that immigrants adjust fully to native norms (assimilation), to more power-aware frameworks that stress the need for native concession (critical), or culturally fluid perspectives that challenge fixed boundaries altogether (constructivist). Co-existence, meanwhile, highlights the persistence of parallel communities with minimal interaction, i.e., a scenario often neglected in policy discussions but highly relevant in urban settings.

Most notably, the illustration identifies a conceptual situation where *mutual adaptation* becomes a focal point. Represented by reciprocal arrows, this situation resonates strongly with CDIM's foundational premise: that integration is not a one-way process, but an interactive and evolving relationship in which both immigrants and natives exert influence. By visualizing these paradigms side by side, the illustration reinforces the need for models that incorporate both the symmetry and the asymmetry inherent in integration dynamics.

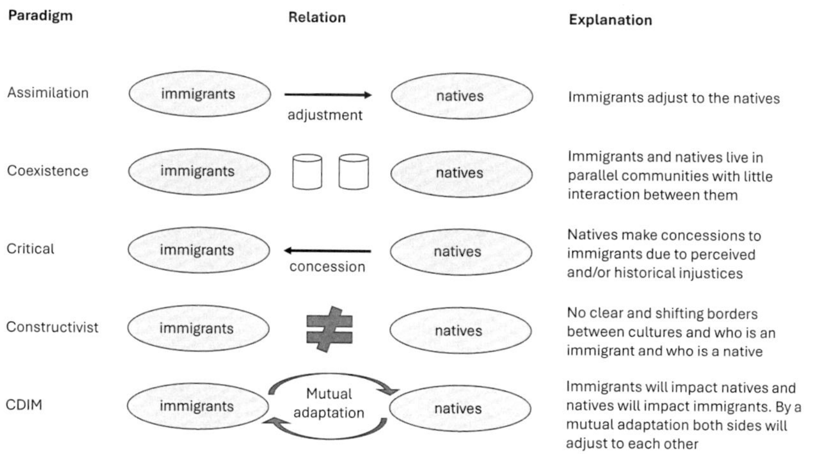

Fig. 7.1 CDIM in comparison to other integration paradigms. Source: Own elaboration

The path ahead demands not merely a choice between existing approaches, but an informed synthesis that bridges the precision offered by mathematical modelling with the nuance foregrounded by critical and constructivist traditions. CDIM provides a scaffold for such theoretical pluralism. However, it requires further development through dialogue across disciplinary boundaries, methodological divides, and experiential perspectives. Bridging quantitative and qualitative approaches will allow integration research to move beyond generalizations and towards deeper, contextually sensitive understandings.

Ultimately, the true value of CDIM will be determined not by its technical sophistication alone, but by its capacity to contribute to *just and effective policies*, i.e., ones that celebrate cultural diversity, foster inclusive communities, and respect the lived experiences of all groups involved. By embracing both formal rigour and sociocultural sensitivity, researchers and policymakers can better navigate the complex terrain of integration, transforming abstract models into tools for meaningful change.

References

Abbott, A. (2004). *Methods of discovery: Heuristics for the social sciences*. W.W. Norton.

Acemoglu, D., & Robinson, J. A. (2012). *Why nations fail: The origins of power, prosperity, and poverty*. Crown Business.

Alba, R., & Nee, V. (2003). *Remaking the American mainstream: Assimilation and contemporary immigration*. Harvard University Press.

Anthias, F. (2013). Intersectional what? Social divisions, intersectionality, and levels of analysis. *Ethnicities, 13*(1), 3–19. https://doi.org/10.1177/1468796812463547

Aoki, M. (2001). *Toward a comparative institutional analysis*. MIT Press.

Barth, F. (1969). *Ethnic groups and boundaries*. Little, Brown & Co.

Bell, D. A. (1987). *And we are not saved: The elusive quest for racial justice*. Basic Books.

Berger, P. L., & Luckmann, T. (1966). *The social construction of reality: A treatise in the sociology of knowledge*. Penguin.

Bhabha, H. K. (1994). *The location of culture*. Routledge.

Bryman, A. (2006). *Quantity and quality in social research*. Routledge.

Cantle, T. (2012). *Interculturalism: The new era of cohesion and diversity*. Palgrave Macmillan.

Castles, S. (2010). Understanding global migration: A social transformation perspective. *Journal of Ethnic and Migration Studies, 36*(10), 1565–1586. https://doi.org/10.1080/1369183X.2010.489381
Crenshaw, K. W. (1991). Mapping the margins: Intersectionality, identity politics, and violence against women of color. *Stanford Law Review, 43*(6), 1241–1299. https://doi.org/10.2307/1229039
Efird, C. R., Wilkins, C. L., & Versey, H. S. (2024). Whiteness hurts society: How whiteness shapes mental, physical, and social health outcomes. *Journal of Social Issues, 80*(1), 53–79.
Esser, H. (2001). Integration und ethnische Schichtung. *Arbeitspapiere-Mannheimer Zentrum für Europäische Sozialforschung, 40*, 1–77.
Favell, A. (2003). Integration nations: The nation-state and research on immigrants in Western Europe. *Comparative Social Research, 22*, 13–42.
Frankenberg, R. (1993). *White women, race matters: The social construction of whiteness*. Routledge.
Geertz, C. (1973). *The interpretation of cultures*. Basic Books.
Golash-Boza, T. (2010). Critical race theory in the US sociology of immigration. *Sociology Compass, 4*(9), 779–789. https://doi.org/10.1111/j.1751-9020.2010.00303.x
Gordon, M. (1964). *Assimilation in American life. The role of race, religion, and national origins*. Oxford University Press.
Greif, A. (2006). *Institutions and the path to the modern economy: Lessons from medieval trade*. Cambridge University Press.
Heckman, J. J. (2000). Causal parameters and policy analysis in economics: A twentieth century retrospective. *Quarterly Journal of Economics, 115*(1), 45–97. https://doi.org/10.1162/003355300554674
Hedström, P., & Bearman, P. (Eds.). (2009). *The Oxford handbook of analytical sociology*. Oxford University Press.
Kymlicka, W. (1996). *Multicultural Citizenship*. Oxford University Press.
Meer, N., & Modood, T. (2012). How does interculturalism contrast with multiculturalism? *Journal of Intercultural Studies, 33*(2), 175–196. https://doi.org/10.1080/07256868.2011.618266
Modood, T. (2007). *Multiculturalism: A Civic Idea*. Polity Press.
North, D. C. (1990). *Institutions, institutional change and economic performance*. Cambridge University Press.
Olcoń, K. (2023). Key concepts in critical whiteness studies. In J. Ravulo, K. Olcoń, T. Dune, A. Workman, & P. Liamputtong (Eds.), *Handbook of critical whiteness*. Springer. https://doi.org/10.1007/978-981-19-1612-0_2-1
Ostrom, E. (2005). *Understanding institutional diversity*. Princeton University Press.
Park, R., & Burgess, E. (1921). *Introduction to the science of sociology*. University of Chicago Press.

Portes, A., & Rumbaut, R. G. (2001). *Legacies: The story of the immigrant second generation*. University of California Press.

Portes, A., & Zhou, M. (1993). The new second generation: Segmented assimilation and its variants. *Annals of the American Academy of Political and Social Science, 530*(1), 74–96. https://doi.org/10.1177/0002716293530001006

Putnam, R. D. (2007). E pluribus unum: Diversity and community in the twenty-first century. *Scandinavian Political Studies, 30*(2), 137–174. https://doi.org/10.1111/j.1467-9477.2007.00176.x

Rauhut, D. (2023). The methodology of immigrant integration: An epistemological perspective. In D. Rauhut (Ed.), *New methods and theory on immigrant integration: Insights from remote and peripheral areas* (pp. 142–162). Edward Elgar Publishing.

Roediger, D. R. (1991). *The wages of whiteness: Race and the making of the American working class*. Verso.

Said, E. W. (1978). *Orientalism*. Pantheon Books.

Spivak, G. C. (1988). Can the subaltern speak? In C. Nelson & L. Grossberg (Eds.), *Marxism and the interpretation of culture* (pp. 271–313). University of Illinois Press.

Vertovec, S. (2007). Super-diversity and its implications. *Ethnic and Racial Studies, 30*(6), 1024–1054. https://doi.org/10.1080/01419870701599465

Williamson, O. E. (2000). The new institutional economics: Taking stock, looking ahead. *Journal of Economic Literature, 38*(3), 595–613. https://doi.org/10.1257/jel.38.3.595

Wimmer, A. (2013). *Ethnic boundary making: Institutions, power, networks*. Oxford University Press.

Wooldridge, J. M. (2010). *Econometric analysis of cross section and panel data* (2nd ed.). MIT Press.

Zapata-Barrero, R. (2016). Theorising intercultural citizenship. In N. Meer, T. Modood, & R. Zapata-Barrero (Eds.), *Multiculturalism and Interculturalism. Debating the dividing lines* (pp. 53–76). Edinburgh University Press.

Zapata-Barrero, R., & Mansouri, F. (2022). A multi-scale approach to Interculturalism: From globalised politics to localised policy and practice. *Journal of International Migration & Integration, 23*(2), 775–795. https://doi.org/10.1007/s12134-021-00846-w

CHAPTER 8

Integration Futures: Where Do We Go from Here?

Reframing Integration: A Summary of Contributions

This monograph has argued that informal institutions, particularly culture, are central to understanding immigrant integration. While integration research has traditionally focused on structural factors such as education, employment, and language acquisition, this work demonstrates that such variables alone cannot account for the persistent challenges observed across generations. Culture, as an informal institution, shapes behavioural expectations, social coordination, and normative legitimacy. It is not a peripheral concern but a foundational determinant of integration outcomes.

Drawing on institutional economics, this study positions culture within the broader architecture of humanly devised constraints that structure interaction (North, 1990). Informal institutions, encompassing norms, values, and preferences, operate alongside formal rules to produce social order. In the context of migration, cultural distance reflects the divergence between the informal institutional frameworks of origin and host societies. This divergence influences not only immigrant adaptation but also host society receptivity, producing what may be termed 'integration friction' (Jones, 2022).

The Cultural Distance Integration Model (CDIM) offers a formalized framework for analysing these dynamics. It conceptualizes cultural distance as a composite of three interrelated layers: civilizational difference

D. Rauhut, *Institutional Economics and Immigrant Integration*,
https://doi.org/10.1007/978-3-032-28361-0_8

(Huntington, 1996), value orientation divergence (Hofstede, 2001), and developmental distance in societal modernization trajectories (Inglehart & Welzel, 2005). CDIM's innovation lies in its capacity to translate these abstract cultural constructs into measurable variables, enabling predictive analysis and policy calibration.

Importantly, CDIM introduces mathematical formalization into a domain where such modelling has been rare. While neoclassical economics routinely employs mathematical tools, institutional economics has tended to favour qualitative and historical analysis. By formalizing cultural distance thresholds and integration dynamics, CDIM bridges this methodological gap, offering a new paradigm for empirical research and policy design.

Integration as Institutional Adaptation

CDIM reframes integration not as a linear process of assimilation or accommodation, but as a complex negotiation between informal institutional systems. Integration succeeds when cultural distance remains within manageable bounds, allowing for mutual adaptation. However, when thresholds are exceeded, i.e., when the divergence in norms, values, and preferences becomes too great, traditional integration strategies lose efficacy. This insight challenges the assumption that integration is merely a matter of time or exposure (see Rauhut, 2020). Instead, it is a function of institutional compatibility.

The model's threshold dynamics reveal that moderate cultural distance may be navigable through standard interventions, but beyond certain tipping points, integration requires more profound institutional recalibration. These thresholds are not arbitrary; they are grounded in the logic of institutional economics, where legitimacy, coordination, and normative alignment are prerequisites for stable social interaction (Greif, 2006; Williamson, 2000).

CDIM also affirms that integration is bidirectional. Host societies must adapt their institutions to accommodate diversity, just as immigrants must navigate new normative landscapes (see Rauhut & Laine, 2023). This reciprocity is essential for sustainable integration and reflects the institutional economics principle that institutions evolve through interaction and feedback (Ostrom, 2005).

Theoretical Innovation

The Cultural Distance Integration Model (CDIM), rooted in institutional economics, offers a distinctive analytical framework for understanding immigrant integration by foregrounding informal institutions, particularly culture, as central explanatory variables. This approach diverges from and complements existing theoretical paradigms, including assimilationist, diversity-oriented, critical, and constructivist perspectives, by introducing a formalized, multi-layered model capable of measuring and predicting integration outcomes based on cultural distance.

Assimilationist theories, such as those advanced by Gordon (1964) and Alba and Nee (2003), posit that integration occurs through the gradual convergence of immigrant and host society norms, often culminating in the absorption of minority cultures into a dominant mainstream. While CDIM acknowledges that cultural proximity can facilitate integration, it challenges the linearity and inevitability assumed in assimilationist models. Instead, CDIM introduces threshold dynamics, demonstrating that integration success depends not merely on time or exposure, but on the degree of institutional compatibility. When cultural distance exceeds certain tipping points, traditional assimilation strategies may fail to produce meaningful outcomes.

Diversity-oriented approaches, including multiculturalist and intercultural frameworks (Kymlicka, 1996; Cantle, 2012), emphasize the value of cultural maintenance and dialogue, advocating for pluralistic societies that accommodate difference. CDIM does not reject these normative commitments but seeks to operationalize them. By quantifying cultural distance and modelling its effects on cognitive, social, and institutional coordination, CDIM provides empirical tools for designing differentiated policies that respect diversity while promoting cohesion. It affirms that equality of opportunity does not require uniformity of intervention, and that tailored responses are essential for equitable integration.

Critical and post-colonial theories, such as those articulated by, e.g., Acheraïou (2008), Fannon (1961), Spivak (1988), Gregory (2004), and Crenshaw (1991), interrogate how integration discourses can reproduce systemic inequalities and mask power asymmetries. These perspectives rightly highlight the political and ideological dimensions of integration policy. CDIM engages these critiques by revealing how cultural distance can be weaponized and used to justify exclusion or pathologize difference. However, CDIM's institutional economics foundation reframes cultural distance not as a moral failing or political construct, but as a measurable constraint on social coordination. This reframing enables policymakers to address integration challenges without resorting to essentialist or discriminatory narratives.

Constructivist theories, including those developed by Barth (1969) and Brubaker (2001), emphasize the fluidity and negotiated nature of cultural identities. CDIM is compatible with this view, recognizing that informal institutions are dynamic and subject to change through interaction. Its bidirectional modelling of adaptation, i.e., where both immigrants and host societies evolve, reflects a constructivist sensibility. Yet CDIM adds analytical precision by identifying the conditions under which such negotiation is likely to succeed or fail, based on the magnitude and nature of cultural distance.

In sum, CDIM does not seek to supplant existing integration theories but to synthesize their insights within a coherent, predictive framework. By grounding integration analysis in institutional economics and introducing mathematical formalization, CDIM advances the field beyond descriptive typologies and normative debates, offering a robust tool for empirical research and policy design.

Practical Policy Implications

From a policy perspective, CDIM offers a suite of tools for evidence-based design and evaluation. By quantifying cultural distance and identifying mechanism-specific challenges, such as cognitive dissonance, coordination failure, and institutional incompatibility, policymakers can tailor interventions to the precise nature of integration friction. This stands in contrast to one-size-fits-all approaches that ignore the cultural profiles of immigrant populations.

CDIM's formalization of threshold dynamics enables policymakers to anticipate when standard measures will fail and to deploy alternative strategies accordingly. For instance, language instruction and employment support may suffice for immigrants from culturally proximate societies but may be inadequate for those from highly divergent backgrounds. Precision policy architecture, informed by CDIM, allows for differentiated responses that respect diversity while promoting cohesion.

The model also supports gender- and class-sensitive programming. Cultural distance is not experienced uniformly; it interacts with social position, gender norms, and educational background. Women from patriarchal societies may face distinct integration barriers, while highly skilled migrants may encounter different forms of institutional misalignment. CDIM's sub-models accommodate these variations, ensuring that integration policy reflects the lived realities of diverse migrant groups.

Furthermore, CDIM introduces spatial dynamics into integration theory. Cultural distance is not only a matter of who we are, but where we live. Spatial clustering of culturally distant populations can amplify integration challenges by reducing intergroup contact and institutional reach. Urban planning, housing policy, and decentralized service provision thus become critical components of integration strategy.

Pathways for Future Research

The CDIM framework opens multiple avenues for scholarly inquiry. Empirical validation is essential. Large-scale datasets such as the World Values Survey and Hofstede's cultural indices provide the foundation for testing CDIM's predictive models across national contexts. Longitudinal studies can explore how cultural distance evolves over time and how generational shifts affect integration trajectories.

Future research should also examine intersectional dimensions of cultural distance. Race, religion, sexual orientation, and disability intersect with cultural norms in complex ways, influencing integration outcomes. Building on Crenshaw's (1991) work on intersectionality and Mirza's (2011) research on disability and migration, CDIM can be extended to model compound forms of institutional friction.

Spatial modelling represents another frontier. Geographic information systems (GIS), ethnographic mapping, and comparative urban studies can elucidate how spatial arrangements mediate cultural distance effects. Integration theory must account for the physical environments in which cultural interaction occurs, recognizing that space shapes opportunity structures and institutional engagement (Rauhut et al., 2023).

Finally, public communication strategies must be developed to present differentiated policy approaches without triggering perceptions of inequity. CDIM's precision can support transparent and legitimate policymaking, fostering informed consent and democratic support.

Navigating Epistemological Tensions

CDIM is unapologetically formal and predictive, grounded in the logic of institutional economics and system modelling. This may contrast with critical paradigms that prioritize narrative, embodiment, and positionality. However, this monograph does not seek to displace alternative approaches. Rather, it offers one mode of inquiry among many, contributing to a pluralistic integration research landscape.

The model's clarity about its aims (prediction, optimization, and policy design) does not preclude engagement with experiential and normative dimensions. On the contrary, CDIM thrives when used alongside constructivist and critical scholarship. Its formal models can identify structural gaps that qualitative research explores in depth, and its predictive tools can highlight outliers that merit ethnographic investigation.

This epistemological reflexivity aligns with Rauhut's (2023) call for methodological pluralism in integration research. By integrating institutional economics with cultural sociology, CDIM offers a shared analytical language capable of bridging disciplinary divides.

Closing Reflection

The Cultural Distance Integration Model equips researchers, policymakers, and practitioners with a conceptual compass and a quantitative toolkit for navigating the complexities of immigrant integration. It moves the discourse from generalizations to gradients, from impressionistic narratives to measurable realities.

Culture is not a soft variable; it is an institutional force. By treating cultural distance as an empirically assessable constraint, CDIM empowers policymakers to act with nuance and urgency. Integration is not achieved through homogenization, but through the orchestration of adaptation (see Rauhut, 2026). This monograph provides the theoretical blueprint, methodological scaffolding, and policy implications to move towards that future.

In a world marked by mobility, hybridity, and contestation over identity, the challenge is not whether difference can be accommodated, but how it must be. CDIM offers a path forward, one that respects complexity, embraces precision, and redefines integration as institutional alignment.

References

Acheraïou, A. (2008). *Rethinking Postcolonialism. Colonialist discourse in modern literatures and the legacy of classical writers.* Palgrave Macmillan.

Alba, R., & Nee, V. (2003). *Remaking the American mainstream: Assimilation and contemporary immigration.* Harvard University Press.

Barth, F. (1969). *Ethnic groups and boundaries.* Little, Brown & Co.

Brubaker, R. (2001). The return of assimilation? Changing perspectives on immigration and its sequels in France, Germany, and the United States. *Journal of Ethnic and Racial Studies, 24*(4), 531–548. https://doi.org/10.1080/01419870120049770

Cantle, T. (2012). *Interculturalism: The new era of cohesion and diversity.* Palgrave Macmillan.

Crenshaw, K. (1991). Mapping the margins: Intersectionality, identity politics, and violence against women of color. *Stanford Law Review, 43*(6), 1241–1299. https://doi.org/10.2307/1229039

Fannon, F. (1961). *The wretched of the earth.* Penguin.

Gordon, M. (1964). *Assimilation in American life. The role of race, religion, and national origins.* Oxford University Press.

Gregory, D. (2004). *The colonial present.* Blackwell.

Greif, A. (2006). *Institutions and the path to the modern economy: Lessons from medieval trade.* Cambridge University Press.

Hofstede, G. (2001). *Culture's consequences: Comparing values, behaviours, institutions and organizations across nations* (2nd ed.). Sage Publications.

Huntington, S. P. (1996). *The clash of civilizations and the remaking of world order.* Simon & Schuster.

Inglehart, R., & Welzel, C. (2005). *Modernization, cultural change, and democracy: The human development sequence.* Cambridge University Press.

Jones, G. (2022). *The culture transplant. How migrants make the economies they move to a lot like the ones they left.* Stanford University Press.

Kymlicka, W. (1996). *Multicultural Citizenship.* Oxford University Press.

Mirza, M. (2011). Disability and migration: A review of the literature. *Social Work in Public Health, 26*(3), 168–180. https://doi.org/10.1080/19371910903519751

North, D. C. (1990). *Institutions, institutional change and economic performance.* Cambridge University Press.

Ostrom, E. (2005). *Understanding institutional diversity.* Princeton University Press.

Rauhut, D. (2020). Integration and informal institutions. *Society, 57*(2), 211–218. https://doi.org/10.1007/s12115-020-00467-6

Rauhut, D. (2023). The methodology of immigrant integration: An epistemological perspective. In D. Rauhut (Ed.), *New methods and theory on immigrant integration: Insights from remote and peripheral areas* (pp. 142–162). Edward Elgar Publishing.

Rauhut, D. (2026). Rethinking immigrant integration theories for the 21st century. In B. Newbold & M. Crea-Arsenio (Eds.), *A research agenda for immigration settlement and adjustment* (pp. 9–29). Edward Elgar.

Rauhut, D., Aigner-Walder, B., & Schomaker, R. (2023). *Economics of immigration beyond the cities*. Palgrave Macmillan.

Rauhut, D., & Laine, J. P. (2023). Crossing the border: Immigrant integration in a bordering perspective. In D. Rauhut (Ed.), *New methods and theory on immigrant integration: Insights from remote and peripheral areas* (pp. 68–85). Edward Elgar.

Spivak, G. C. (1988). Can the subaltern speak? In C. Nelson & L. Grossberg (Eds.), *Marxism and the interpretation of culture* (pp. 24–28). Macmillan.

Williamson, O. E. (2000). The new institutional economics: Taking stock, looking ahead. *Journal of Economic Literature, 38*(3), 595–613. https://doi.org/10.1257/jel.38.3.595

Index[1]

[1] Note: Page numbers followed by 'n' refer to notes.

D. Rauhut, *Institutional Economics and Immigrant Integration*, https://doi.org/10.1007/978-3-032-28361-0

MIX
Papier | Fördert
gute Waldnutzung
FSC® C083411

Zeitfracht Medien GmbH
Ferdinand-Jühlke-Straße 7
99095 Erfurt, Deutschland
produktsicherheit@kolibri360.de